Leadership

The Power of Character

Robert L. Vernon

First published in the United States of America
By Robert L. Vernon
Revised November 2013
© 2003 Robert L. Vernon
Originally Published as:
"Eight Ethics of Highly Effective Leaders"

All rights reserved. No part of this publication may be reproduced, stored in a retrieval system, or transmitted in any form or by any means, electronic, mechanical, photocopying, recording, or otherwise, without the prior permission of the copyright owner.

Robert L. Vernon
P.O. Box 392
Bonsall, California 92003
United States of America

Preface

What makes a powerful leader? Is it something inherited? Is it learned behavior? Can anyone acquire leadership abilities with sufficient determination? Why do some people seem to have a "presence" that compels others to follow? What is it about them that give them a powerful ability to influence others?

These questions have been asked for centuries. Yet the answers are clear. Powerful leaders do have some behaviors and characteristics in common. What may seem to be a mystery can be understood.

This book documents a strong consensus about leadership behavior, discovered as I traveled to over 30 countries conducting seminars for military, police, and political leaders. Once these behaviors were documented, people from all walks of life confirmed that these behaviors work well in any situation where one desires to influence others. Leaders from all of the countries involved in building this consensus recognized that these behaviors are rarely practiced consistently. I discovered that these behaviors were connected to the issue of character. My focus then shifted to ethics and character. An examination of literature, practical experience, and continued interaction with world leaders led to the identification of eight essential character traits.

This book reveals the essential character traits (or ethics) that result in powerful leadership behavior. Rather than merely addressing behavior, I probed deeper to identify, discuss, and practically apply the whole issue of character.

Leadership – the power of character

Leadership – the power of character

Table of Contents

Introduction 1

Part 1 Defining Leadership

Chapter 1 Leadership vs. Management 7
Chapter 2 Born Leaders 17
Chapter 3 Behaviors of Effective Leaders 21
Chapter 4 The Necessity of Foundation 39

Part 2 Eight Core Character Traits

Chapter 5 Integrity 47
Chapter 6 Courage 59
Chapter 7 Discipline 67
Chapter 8 Loyalty 75
Chapter 9 Diligence 87
Chapter 10 Humility 95
Chapter 11 Optimism 107
Chapter 12 Conviction 117

Part 3 Principles in An Organization

Chapter 13 Principle-Based Leadership 129
Chapter 14 Organizational Lifecycle 139
Chapter 15 Steps of Leadership 153
Chapter 16 Core Beliefs 161
Chapter 17 Ten Ancient Principles 167
Chapter 18 The Spiritual Dimension of Leadership 177

Appendix 185

Leadership – the power of character

Introduction

Shortly after retiring from the Los Angeles Police Department (LAPD), I was invited to lecture at the University of Switzerland in Bern. Near the end of our stay, Heinrich Minder, a Swiss businessman, asked if I would speak to members of the Hungarian Parliament. It turned out that this would also afford me an opportunity to visit Prague, Czechoslovakia, which was the closest city to the family home of my mother.

While waiting to clear customs, we met Geoff Skippage, a retired British military officer who was in Prague to meet with heads of the Czech military about doing an ethics seminar. We asked if we could tag along, and soon after, we were sitting with three generals in a conference room

After a few opening greetings, Skippage asked the military leaders, "Have you given up the philosophy of dialectical materialism that supports communism?"

"Yes," the leaders agreed, "that philosophy died with the peaceful revolution."

"May I ask what you have replaced it with?"

The leaders looked at each other, shrugged their shoulders, and one answered, "We haven't replaced it with anything."

Skippage seemed to anticipate that answer and immediately asked, "Have you considered the Christian ethic and philosophy?"

The leader of the threesome spread his hands and said, "We'd like to if we only understood it."

Again Skippage had anticipated this answer, and he proceeded to present them with a brochure about his seminar on Christian ethics, designed for military leaders. Within the brochure were pictures taken at a seminar in Moscow. The generals recognized several of their Russian counterparts. This set off an animated discussion among the three men while we watched and waited. I could imagine their discussion. They hated the nation that had once dominated their country, yet they respected its power. If Russian generals needed this seminar, then maybe Czech leadership needed it too. By a vote of two to one, Skippage left the meeting with permission to return and teach the seminar.

It was late morning as we prepared to leave the building, allowing me a few hours to tour the city and search for my roots. But as we emerged from the military headquarters, several police cars with lights flashing blocked my exit. One of the uniformed men approached me and in accented English asked, "Are you Robert Vernon?"

"Yes, sir."

"Come with us, please."

Minder and I were then escorted to a waiting car, and with police cars before and behind us, we began a rapid ride through Prague. "Where are we going?" I asked my interpreter.

"Stanislav Novotny wants to see you. He is Prezident (sic) of the Czech police."

Minder then admitted, "I told them about you."

We drove into the driveway of the police presidium, our doors were opened, and we were led to an elevator that took us to the fourth floor where we were ushered into Novotny's office. Along the way, my interpreter explained that the president of the national police was a colleague of Czech president Vaclav Havel.

As we entered the "Prezident's" office, Minder stated, "The proposal Geoff made to the military, you will make to the police."

"Do you mean to teach an ethics seminar? But I have no seminar."

Minder smiled and said, "Make the proposal, and then prepare the seminar."

Novotny invited us to sit around his conference table and after offering us beverages told how police had beaten him in Wenseslas Square during one of the demonstrations that had led to the peaceful overthrow of the communist regime. "I nearly died because of the police," he said, leaning back in his chair. Then with a gesture, he said; "Now I'm their leader! I am responsible for all 24,000 police in the country."

I briefly explained my Czech heritage through my mother.

Then Novotny invited me to speak. Having no better idea of what to say, I asked him a question, "Have you given up the philosophy of dialectic materialism that supports communism?"

Novotny leaned forward, folded his hands, and gazed into my eyes. "Yes, completely," he answered.

I could see friendship in his eyes and warm openness. His smile was genuine; his interest sincere.

"Have you considered replacing it with Christian ethics and philosophy?"

"I would like to. The police need something to replace the old ways. Do you have anything in writing that I can consider?"

"No, I don't," I admitted. "However, I will send you a proposal for a training seminar for your police chiefs as soon as I get home."

I sent Novotny a proposal to train fifty of his leadership team. A few months later, I was faxed an invitation to train one hundred of his police chiefs in the ethics of leadership. Not to be outdone, other former totalitarian countries—Hungary, Mongolia, Albania, and Russia quickly issued invitations to train their police chiefs as well. Other countries followed as well so that I had to quickly recruit others to help handle the invitations.

This book contains the essence of what I've learned and taught around the world. I have discovered that all effective leaders share basically the same qualities—that is, all leaders that people desire to follow. For many countries that have only known harsh dictatorships, the change to democratic leadership has been traumatic. How do you cause people to desire to follow you, rather than forcing them to follow?

The problem that I have discovered is that most people in authority confuse the concept of control with true leadership. During the communist dictatorship, the style of leadership was autocratic control. Threats, violence, and other means of force were used to get the people to do what was wanted. True leadership was not practiced. Rather, a system of despotic control and manipulation was utilized. After the collapse of the Soviet Empire, governmental leaders found they lacked the skills of convincing people to move in the desired direction.

A similar phenomenon has occurred in the West. Although the contrasts are not as pronounced, a change has transpired in the way organizations are governed. During most of the period referred to as the Industrial Revolution or "second wave" described by Alvin Toffler in *The Third Wave* (Bantam Books, 1981), leaders of organizations had authority that was nearly absolute. They did not utilize the violence or terror employed in countries where tyranny reigned. But they did have the power to dictate the behavior of workers who wanted to remain in their employ. Many forces have mandated a change in the relationship between the boss and the worker or the leader and those who follow.

The rise of the union movement began to erode the absolute power exercised by management. Legislative action and court decisions further diminished the power and authority of those in power. The expansion of administrative law continued the evolution of "workers' rights." In family or juvenile courts, "children's rights" have diminished parental authority. In short, there is no authority that is above challenge or resistance.

Consequently, the seminars designed for the dramatic change in the Eastern Bloc countries are now being presented in the United States and other Western countries. Heads of governmental agencies and private organizations in democratic countries now see a need to develop an approach to leadership that depends less on absolute power and more on inspiration, motivation, and empowerment. A whole new paradigm is upon us. True leadership has become relevant for this new age.

A major thesis emerged about leadership based upon the knowledge gained through participating in the seminars, researching literature, and considering real-life experiences. This thesis has three important components:

(1) Leadership is different from classical management and/or management theory;

(2) There are observable behaviors that are commonly recognized throughout the world as necessary in order for true inspirational leadership to occur;

(3) Most importantly, these behaviors cannot be sustained without a foundation of character and ethics.

This book addresses this thesis and all of its components. The behaviors recognized worldwide as mandatory for inspirational leadership will be identified. Most importantly, the ethics or character traits that support these behaviors will be described and discussed. This book will go beyond addressing the skills and actions commonly connected with leadership; it will penetrate behavior to the level of attitudes and character. If you are interested in effectively influencing others, this book is for you.

Defining Leadership

Chapter 1
Leadership vs. Management

The crisis of our times is leadership. The crisis in leadership is character. We want to believe that leadership involves power, prestige, respect, and special privileges. We have images of all of these things automatically being conferred upon us if we are just given a title, position, or simply declare ourselves *Leader.*

Leadership is somewhat like health. It is not something you can demand, claim, or have conferred upon you. To a great extent, I believe a person's health is a result of eating the right foods, maintaining an exercise program, keeping appropriate sleeping patterns, and of course inheriting good genes. While we do not choose our genes, we do make choices about our living patterns. These choices reflect character traits—traits like discipline and diligence. Likewise, leadership is the result of specific character traits and the resulting actions. The attributes of a good leader, such as respect, authority, and credibility, are not things that can be conferred upon or given to an individual. They must be earned.

Much is known about leadership. We live in a time when there are more books, films, and videos about leadership than ever before. In 2002, the Internet bookstore giant Amazon.com listed over eight thousand leadership titles. Yet many authorities agree there is a crisis or vacuum of true leadership in our world. Leadership and how to get it are issues that are greatly misunderstood.

Why the vacuum? Why the crisis? I believe we can discover the answers to these questions. Much of the leadership materials today are directed toward running a business or enterprise. They address classic management techniques such as planning, organizing, staffing, budgeting, coordinating, directing, and researching. No question, these are important topics. Competent management activities are necessary for running any organization. However, those activities do not, in themselves, constitute real leadership.

Leadership: The Power of Character

This book is about leadership, not management. Both are needed for a group of people to become effective and achieve excellence. They are related concepts, but they are distinct and different. Warren Bennis makes the following insightful comparisons:

Managers	**Leaders**
Administer	Innovate
Maintain	Develop
Focus on systems and structure	Focus on people
Rely on control	Inspire trust
Ask how and when	Ask what and why
Initiate	Originate
Do things right	Do the right things[1]

In June of 1995, I was in Budapest with members of our European team presenting a leadership seminar to the top executives of the Hungarian Police. Near the beginning of the three-day seminar we noticed that many of the participants were reacting negatively to the term *leadership*. They seemed confused about the context surrounding our use of this word. I assumed that there was a breakdown in communication—either our translators were not accurate in performing their duties, or there was a problem with the word itself.

I interrupted my presentation and asked the participants to define what the word *leadership* meant to them. Even before the translator completed the translation, I heard several participants say, "Stalin."

One of the police chiefs rose to explain, "Stalin chose the word *Leader* as his title. And what was leadership to him? Brutal terrorism! He was a despot!" Others in the room agreed with that assessment. "He was cruel and oppressive. That's not the leadership we want," said one.

---

[1] Warren Bennis, *On Becoming a Leader* (Add city: Addison-Wesley, 1989), 45.

This incident was a reminder that the powerful word *leadership* has different connotations to various people. For some it is positive, reflecting some individual they want to follow. But for many, the term is extremely negative, conjuring up images of unacceptable, cruel, and oppressive incidents. For my audience, which had only recently escaped from the oppression of communism, Stalin was a man who had every possible tool of power at his disposal, yet he was despised. These officers might have been forced to yield to Stalin's authority, but they would never willingly follow him.

Defining Terms

I believe there is also confusion about leadership in democratic countries. Being in a position of leadership can stimulate egocentric motives and behavior. As illustrated, deception is most likely to occur when the person deceived is in on the deception—that is, when he or she deeply desires the results of the deception. For example, so-called con men play on the "larceny in everyone" to make their swindle or racket work. Well-educated and stable people can be drawn into swindle schemes that have a blatantly ridiculous premise. Likewise, a person's ego can draw them into a faulty view of leadership.

The following definition is not meant to be exhaustive or technical. Its purpose is to help communicate what I mean when I use the word in this book. For this limited purpose, I have chosen to define leadership with five statements.

Leadership—

1. The ability to clearly understand and articulate the goal

2. The confidence to be out in front and show the way to the goal

3. The ability to convince people to follow as an act of their free choice

4. The desire and ability to help people develop and pursue excellence

5. The capability to inspire people to achieve their full potential

1. The ability to clearly *understand* and *articulate* the goal
Leadership is intertwined with the concept of goals. The word *lead* itself indicates movement. It can be actual physical movement or movement of a more esoteric nature. To lead implies that there is a direction or a choice of alternative directions in which to move. Perhaps there is a perceived need to move from a static state to action. Or there may be a desire to move from a certain level of accomplishment to a higher one. It can involve movement from one philosophy to another or from one strategy to another. But it involves movement of some type. People who are successful as leaders know where they are going. They have a clearly defined objective that they have a *passion* to achieve.

> "All leaders have the capacity to create a compelling vision."
> Warren Bennis

Leaders are motivated for some reason to convince others to achieve certain goals. Effective leaders have the ability to *conceptualize* goals and then *communicate* the goals to others in a clearly understandable way. They communicate goals in such a way that the goals seem desirable and worthwhile to pursue. They also have the insight to distinguish between goals and strategies and/or tactics that are intended to achieve the goals.

In order to reach a goal, one must clearly understand what the goal is. Understanding a goal brings meaning and sense to actions, tactics, and strategies intended to reach the goal. Therefore a leader must (1) have the ability to clearly identify specific goals, (2) have the skills to effectively communicate the goals to others, (3) secure the commitment of those being led to pursue the goals, and finally (4) maintain *focus* on those goals. These four abilities and/or skills sound simple and straightforward. They are not. Each involves a strong commitment and plenty of hard work.

2. The confidence to be out in front and show the way to the goal

Leadership involves commitment. Effective leaders exude the confidence that they are leading their followers in the right direction. (See chapter 11 on Conviction.) By demonstrating confidence, the leader gives assurance to those being led that they are moving in the right direction and that their goal is achievable. A very powerful way to demonstrate this confidence is to model the desired action. In other words, lead by example. *Leading by example is the most powerful way to lead.*

> "The first great gift we can bestow on others is a good example."
> Thomas Morell

Confidence does not just happen. It is not the result of doing what comes naturally. Confidence is the result of doing one's homework. People who have a confident opinion about a particular subject or issue are usually well aware of facts and data about the issue. Often they have researched the issue thoroughly. Their confidence is based upon a factual analysis and/or well-developed reason. By taking the action he or she is asking others to do, a leader demonstrates the confidence that the action is worthwhile, possible to accomplish, and a good course of action.

> "Doubt whom you will, But never yourself."
> Christian Nestell Bovee

3. The ability to convince people to follow as an act of their free choice

This is one of the dimensions that contrasts leadership with management. Leadership involves salesmanship. Not an insincere "snow job" to manipulate people, but a personal conviction that translates into persuasion and influence. True leadership implies that those being led follow *because they want to.* Something powerful has happened. The leader has provided a combination of information, training, logic, challenge, hope—something that has caused those being led to follow as an act of their own will. They perform the desired action or strive to achieve the goal because they have "bought into it." This form of positive influence is the opposite of autocratic control often associated with management that resorts to mandates, pressure, intimidation, and force.

> *"It's not called the 'art of persuasion' for nothing.*
> *This intangible, often elusive, skill was a mainstay*
> *in Lincoln's interaction arsenal."*[2]

One of the essential behaviors to model is that of following. If leading by example is the most powerful way to lead (and it is), then the leader must first and foremost be a follower. A leader must demonstrate his or her commitment to following the higher authority, such as the CEO, a board of directors, the law, or the government. (See chapter 7 on Loyalty.)

4. The desire and ability to help people develop and pursue excellence

True leadership means becoming a servant. It must involve helping people do their tasks well. In this kind of direction, the leader does not see the individuals that he or she is trying to lead as a means to an end, but rather as a major part of the end. This leader sees those being led as fellow human beings that have similar dreams, aspirations, and needs. He or she knows that the achievement of excellence brings fulfillment and that fulfillment continues the cycle leading to higher levels of accomplishment and excellence.

When I commanded five of LAPD's eighteen geographical police stations, I conducted an experiment. I had the commanding officer of one of those

---

[2] Donald T. Phillips, *Lincoln on Leadership* (Add city: Warner Books, 1992), 47

stations train his first level supervisors (Sergeants) to discover the aspirations of their respective squad members (8 to 12 each). They asked two basic questions: (1) "Where do you want to be five years from now on this department (their dreams or goals)? (2) "How can I help you get there?" Sadly, one officer reported that in his fifteen years on the department this was the first time anyone had shown an interest in his future. He explained that he was pleased that he now had someone working with him to help him realize his dream of becoming a homicide detective before his career ended. The results of that exercise were a noticeable improvement of productivity and overall effectiveness of that Division.

Successful leaders demonstrate a genuine interest in their followers. They make an effort to get to know their followers personally. They do intrude inappropriately into their personal lives; but they do make themselves available to encourage and assist them in achieving their personal goals.

From a practical standpoint, a person cannot be led to perform an act that he or she is incapable of doing. Leadership therefore includes preparing people to perform the tasks that are necessary to reach the goal. It involves equipping them with the skills, tools, technology, and other resources they will need to be successful. It also involves removing or minimizing barriers to goal achievement.

*" . . . effectiveness comes about through
enabling others to reach their potential"* [3]

5. The capability to inspire people to achieve their full potential

Inspiration is more powerful than *motivation*. Motivation works when the boss is watching or there is a good chance he or she will become aware of the follower's behavior. Motivation is external and usually involves a reward and/or a sanction. On the other hand, inspiration comes from within. Somehow the leader has

---

[3] Max Depree, *Leadership Is an Art* (Add city: Dell Publishing, 1989), 19

penetrated through the follower's logic all the way to their heart. Leadership involves influencing people's attitudes and actions. Therefore, effective leaders have the desire and capability to inspire people. Their confidence, enthusiasm, and total commitment are obvious, and therefore they are contagious.

To be able to inspire others, leaders must themselves be inspired. They must have a high level of sincerity and excitement about the mission. Many executives and supervisors can motivate people, but few can inspire them. People have almost unlimited potential when they are inspired, especially when working together as a team. Good leaders know that and work diligently to lift up the standard to a high level. They challenge people to reach for that high standard and somehow are able to instill in them the belief that they can reach it.

Inspiration involves touching the very core beliefs of a person. Inspiration penetrates through the intellect to the emotions. Inspiration touches a person's attitudes. A person becomes impassioned about something upon which they place high value. Therefore effective leaders emphasize principle and matters of conviction.

> *"A gifted leader is one who is able to touch your heart."*
> — J.S. Potofsky

Summary

One of the trends in our culture is the deterioration of absolute authority. Extreme individualism has eroded the power once held by heads of corporations, teachers in the classroom, certain governmental officials, and even parents in the home. In short, traditional authority is being challenged, assaulted, and deteriorated. This phenomenon mandates an understanding and application of true leadership.

The confusion I found about leadership in the former communist countries of Eastern Europe isn't unique; it exists in democratic countries as well. Being in a position of leadership can stimulate egocentric motives and behavior. Such leaders deceive themselves when they believe this is genuine leadership. That is why we need to step back and examine the *behaviors* of effective leaders. When we take the focus off our desire to be a leader and instead focus on what kind of leaders we desire to follow, we gain much needed perspective.

I have found that when a leader (1) clearly develops valuable goals; (2) models the pursuit of those goals; (3) prepares and equips the followers to also pursue those goals; and (4) inspires the followers by making the goals noble, meaningful and worthy to achieve; the followers will choose to follow as an act of their free choice

Plan for success:

1. Describe several specific actions you can take to improve your orientation to goals and your ability to explain them to others.
2. Outline several specific ways you can improve your role model to those you intend to influence.
3. Describe several ways you can demonstrate your commitment to help your followers achieve their personal goals in life.

Leadership: The Power of Character

Chapter 2
Born Leaders

Unequal endowments

There is a long standing debate about the source of leadership ability. Are certain people born with effective leadership skills; or are these skills the result of a development process? I believe there is truth to both sides of this argument.

Certain people do seem to be "natural leaders." Often their leadership ability emerges at a very early age, long before they are exposed to education or training. Some would argue that although it may appear to be "on the genes," these individuals have actually picked up leadership traits in their early years from the family setting and example. These are the so-called environmentalists. This explanation does not explain why siblings from the exact same family environment are so different in leadership abilities. I believe leadership traits can be inherited. I believe certain personality traits can be ingrained on the DNA that forms personality.

Having said that, I have also observed people develop into leaders. I have observed many individuals with little "natural" leadership skills become effective leaders. These are people who either though necessity or strong desire work diligently at developing the skills and behavior they need to influence others.

Essentially, I believe that we are all born with various levels of leadership potential. Some are born with a large container or package of leadership potential. Others begin life with a much smaller potential. Envision two canteens left for travelers at a desert location. One is a gallon container but only has eight (8) ounces of water in it. The other is a quart container; but is brim full of fresh water. If you were dying of thirst and had to choose one of these vessels, which would it be? The point is that some people with great leadership potential, waste that potential. They do not pursue their full potential in this regard. Others with less potential have done their best to "fill" their smaller container to the brim.

I believe that almost everyone who truly desires to influence or lead others can develop the capacity to do so. Some will have to work harder at it than others; but I strongly believe that leadership can be understood and nurtured.

Lack of Opportunity

Many people complain about the lack of opportunity to lead. They argue that if they were just given a chance to lead, they could and would. These folk seem to be waiting for someone to hand them a spectacular position of leadership on the proverbial silver platter. I have found that one of the distinguishing characteristics of leaders is that they look diligently for opportunities to lead. They have the drive and ability to spot leadership opportunities, or create them. Leaders do not wait for leadership to come to them – they pursue it

Individual committed to leadership often pursue the opportunity to lead in less than obvious situations. For example, some look at a crisis as a dangerous opportunity to lead. When facing a crisis, everyone is usually looking for a way out. Leaders seize the initiative and offer the solution to the problem. They attack the crisis. Even if they do not have the positional power to lead, they suggest alternatives to those that do. Is so doing, they are seen as problem solvers and are often place in a position of leadership.

Opportunities to lead are all around us. I am convinced that everyone is surrounded by these opportunities. The big difference between leaders and followers regarding opportunities is twofold: (1) They recognize opportunities as such; and (2) they have the courage to seize the initiative.

Motives of leaders

The motives of those seeking a leadership role are relevant. Knowing and understanding your own motives for seeking an exercising leadership is important. Many pursue leadership out of pride and selfish ambition. They see a leadership role as leading to recognition, accolades and praise. Some seek leadership to push a personal agenda. Often the motive is simply power. To some people, power is everything.

The motives underlying a leader's actions and decisions eventually become known. It is possible to conceal one's motives only temporarily. Generally the size of the group being led has a relationship to the length of time it takes for a leader's motives to become known. Where the group being led is small and has daily contact with the leader, the exposure time is usually short. In a situation where the group being led is large and few have close contact with the leader, the exposure time can be lengthy. Nevertheless, in either case the leader's motives will eventually emerge.

Followers are more likely to follow a leader when they believe that the motives of the leader are noble and in their best interests. They appreciate decisions and actions based upon motives of integrity, fairness, professionalism, loyalty and morality. Conversely, they despise leaders who make decisions based solely upon what will make the leader look good. They detest leaders who "throw followers under the bus" in order to advance their own career.

Two thousand years ago, the Apostle Paul wrote about the importance of motives in defending his own leadership: *". . . wait until the Lord comes who will both bring to light the things hidden in the darkness and disclose the motives of men's hearts"* . [4]

Followers expend themselves to produce good results for a leader whose motives are selfless. Ultimately a leader whose motives are self-sacrificing will get the recognition, praise and rewards they richly deserve.

---

[4] The New American Standard Bible: (Foundation Press, La Habra, CA. 1960) 1 Corinthians 4:5

Summary

People are endowed with various levels of leadership traits. Leadership traits can also be discovered and nurtured. Those with a high level of natural leadership traits will not necessarily emerge as a great leader. They may not exercise the courage to seize the initiative. Or they may have a self centered motive for their leadership that turns others away. People emerge as great leaders primarily because they recognize all of the factors bearing on true leadership. They choose to fill their inborn vessel of leadership potential to the brim. They study leadership. They look for opportunities. They choose to override their fears with the courage to seize the initiative. Finally, they strive to maintain a motive that will encourage their followers.

Plan for success:

1. Describe several specific actions you can take to improve your understanding and application of leadership principles (i.e. study books, attend seminars, interview respected leaders)
2. Outline several specific actions you plan to take to be more aware of leadership opportunities. What crisis do you or your organization face that can be turned into an opportunity to lead?
3. Describe your present motives behind your desire to lead. Revise those motives, where appropriate, so they will be perceived by your followers as more focused on serving them.

Chapter 3
Behaviors of Effective Leaders

During the last three decades that I have taught and/or facilitated seminars on the topic of leadership, I have asked literally thousands of mid- and upper-management people the same question. I have asked them to define the ideal leader—in terms of *behavior.* These exercises have been conducted in a variety of settings both in the USA and abroad. They have involved a demographic mixture of men and women. Yet there has been an amazing consistency of response.

In fact, the answers are so consistent that I have prepared computer generated PowerPoint presentations in the language of the attendees with the answers I know I will get from my audience. The attendees are usually somewhat startled to find that their opinions about leadership behavior are virtually identical from group to group and country to country. Different words or phrases are used, but they communicate the same ideas or concepts across geographic, socio-economic, racial, and cultural lines. In the following chapter, we will describe the behaviors that most commonly surface as a result of the process I have defined.

Interestingly, this list also describes the leader I have chosen as the most effective leader in my thirty eight year career with the L.A.P.D. His name is Tom Janes. He led more through inspiration than raw power. As I look back on my time under him, I realize that every one of the leadership behaviors identified by my classes worldwide were qualities he exhibited. I believe that is why he was recognized by his peers and by all that worked for him as the ideal leader. So here they are. The behavior patterns that followers rate as most important in their leader.

The most desired behavior patterns in effective leaders

1) An Effective Leader Is Decisive

I once worked with a high-level executive that was actually proud of his ability to avoid making decisions. One day, he showed me a drawer in his desk that he had set aside to store difficult decisions. "Here's how it works," he explained. "All proposals, requests for approval, and any other documentation or information I might need is locked in this drawer. No one, not even my secretaries or executive assistants, have access to this drawer." The executive showed me various decisions he was being asked to make, then laughed as he said, "You know, most decisions have a way of resolving themselves. I keep these files for thirty days. Most of them don't need any decision by the end of that period."

This man was partially correct—the issues in his drawer were resolved, but rarely by themselves. He forced others to assume his responsibility to confront issues and make decisions that were truly matters within his purview. The amazing thing was that he did not see this as a deficiency on his part. He was actually proud of this method of avoiding responsibility. He didn't realize that his staff had no respect for him.

Avoiding decisions is one of the most common complaints I hear about supervisors and executives. People do not enjoy following someone who is unwilling to bite the bullet and make tough decisions. They recognize that failure to make a decision *is a decision*. Usually, this means that the indecisive leader doesn't want the responsibility of the decision. He wants instead to push it on someone else.

I am not advocating being impulsive or making decisions without due consideration. Good decisions are based upon facts, input from others, and due deliberation. However, I have seen many people in authority go overboard in seeking information. Some bosses repeatedly kick back suggestions or recommendations from their followers, requesting more information. This can be a way to avoid a decision. Having all of the information on a pending issue is not a decision—it is a conclusion.

People like to follow someone who is decisive, and that was certainly true of Tom Janes. He never made a decision by avoiding a decision. But his decisiveness went further; he made his expectations very clear. We knew how he would evaluate us and what he considered success and failure in our jobs. When we followed his leadership, he backed us up. Thus, decisions were made in a timely fashion, and he took full responsibility for their effect.

> *"Nothing is more difficult, and therefore more precious, than being able to decide".*
> Napolean Bonaparte

The reality is that when someone makes a clear decision *and makes that decision public,* they run the risk of being wrong. Thus, being decisive can be costly. Decisive leaders face the possibility of being proven in error and/or unpopular or politically incorrect because a decisive person presents a tangible record to observe and evaluate. Decisions also reveal beliefs and values. Leaders who are not sure of their principles or absolutes, or are embarrassed by them, naturally prefer they not be exposed. But in the process, they lose the respect of their followers.

2) An Effective Leader Is a Good Listener

People like to work with a leader who will listen to their opinions and suggestions. We know intuitively that the more information a leader has, the more likely he or she will provide good leadership. Respondents in my survey have recorded that they are more willing to follow someone who will give their input a fair evaluation. They explain that they do not expect the leader to always follow their suggestions or recommendations but they do appreciate an openness to receive and evaluate them.

What makes this tricky for some leaders is that often someone lower in the hierarchy has more experience in a particular field than the person in a leadership position. That person knows the leader could benefit from his or her insight if given the opportunity to state it. People in this situation usually want to give their opinion—and will do so, if they sense the decision maker will give them a fair hearing.

Early in my career in law enforcement, I was sent to a supervisory school to prepare for my promotion to sergeant. I vividly recall a visual aid used by one of the instructors—a series of cartoons representing the various levels of power in any organization. The individual at the lowest level of power had huge ears and practically no mouth. At each successive step upward, a strange transformation took place—the character's mouth became bigger and the ears smaller. The point was obvious. The normal tendency is to listen less and talk more as one gains power. Although normal, it is actually dysfunctional.

Leaders who are responsive to those they lead model the behavior they want from their followers. Leaders want their followers to be responsive. The most powerful way to obtain this cooperative spirit is to demonstrate it. This attitude of responsiveness is part of a leadership style coined *servant leadership.*

Many leaders recognize the value of "management by walking around." Some value a so-called "open door" policy. These and other similar techniques acknowledge the importance of listening to others. But there is a big danger in these practices. Listening without responding will reduce a leader's effectiveness. Obtaining feedback from customers, constituents, or followers without reacting actually erodes a leader's credibility. People are inspired by a leader that they sense cares for them and wants to do something about their problems. Being responsive is a powerful way to demonstrate respect and prove you really care.

Effective listening requires great skill. First and foremost it requires a *desire* on the part of the listener to receive information. Leaders reveal their attitude about listening to subordinates in a variety of ways. More will be said about this later. At this point, suffice it to say that being a good listener is one of the first-noted and highest-valued leadership behaviors.

Leadership: The Power of Character

> *"A good listener is not only popular everywhere, but after a while he knows something."*
> Wilson Mizner

3) An Effective Leader Keeps Commitments

Respondents described this behavior in many ways. Some stated they enjoy following someone who does not withdraw their support when an approved action is criticized. Others described their fear of having their boss actually deny knowledge of approved strategies or tactics that are later determined to be inappropriate.

When a leader asks his or her followers to pursue a course of action, there is often an agreement that certain conditions will be met. For example, the leader may assure the followers they will be given specific resources, training, and/or compensation. The respondents explained that when these conditions are not met, trust erodes, and future motivation is compromised.

The issue of keeping commitments is important in all leadership situations, but it is especially important in settings where the stakes are high. For example, in my profession it is extremely important for followers to know that a leader will keep his word when supporting or ordering the use of force. A sniper directed to use deadly force against a life-threatening criminal must be absolutely certain that his commander will accept responsibility for that decision when the inevitable criticism begins. A financial officer must be certain that direction from his boss involving millions of dollars will not be disavowed if there is a failure.

There is a traditional saying that applies here, "Fool me once—shame on you; Fool me twice—shame on me." A leader who is not diligent in keeping commitments may be effective for a brief period of time, but those who follow this path soon lose their credibility. Credibility is necessary for effective long-term leadership.

4) An Effective Leader Gives Recognition

A few months after going to work as a lieutenant in Accident Investigation, I was driving up Interstate 5 to dinner one evening when I saw a plume of black smoke in the vicinity of Dodger Stadium. I quickly put on my lights, exited the freeway, and pulled up to a helicopter that had crashed and was blazing. One officer had arrived ahead of me and was trying to pull someone out of the wreckage, although I could tell the occupant was already dead. I called headquarters for ambulances. Meanwhile, a bystander came running to my car, shouting, "There's another helicopter down on the hill by the stadium."

I rolled quickly to that scene and recognized by the paint scheme that it was a police chopper. I reached for the mike and keyed the switch.

"T–10 to control."

"T–10, go."

"T–10, do we have any air units up?"

"T–10, that's a roger. Air three is clear."

"T–10, please see if you can make contact."

"Air three, come in. . . Air three, code one."

There was only silence, and I knew that the worst had happened. I secured the area and set up the command post. It was a long night, made harder by the fact that I was inexperienced in accident investigations. One sergeant on my crew was very helpful and made some important suggestions, which I followed. Later, the FAA commended our process, and I knew I needed to recognize the good thinking and timely actions of this sergeant.

It was after midnight as we were finishing our work. Tom Janes was now on the scene, and I told him about the sergeant. "I need to go find him and thank him for his diligence and initiative demonstrated during this investigation."

"No," Tom said, "not now." I looked at him in surprise. "He is alone. Wait and do it publicly, in front of his peers and subordinates."

"Like at role call tomorrow?" I asked.

"Yes, that's perfect. Do it then."

As a rising leader, I knew granting recognition was important. But Tom did this intentionally, thinking about when recognition would have the greatest effect on the one being praised. While respondents indicated a variety of opinions of how this should be done, the value of recognition is a universally valued behavior around the world. This seems to be true regardless of one's position, education, or level of sophistication.

> *"I can live for two months on a compliment."*
> Mark Twain

People have a need to feel significant, and effective leaders recognize this as a powerful motivator. Receiving public recognition seems to be one of the roads to significance, especially when focused upon the character traits foundational to behavior. Leaders err in either granting too little or too much recognition. It is easy to see the problem of a leader who ignores this important function. The opposite is also true. When recognition is overdone or focuses only upon behavior and not character, the process is cheapened. A leader must use good judgment in selecting the appropriate level of recognition for each demonstration of character.

The old adage "Chew out in private; praise in public" is appropriate at this point. It is best to reserve ceremonial types of recognition for those acts that are truly above and beyond the ordinary. However, informal or even casual "atta boys" are hard to overdo. The simple act of telling someone in the presence of their peers that you appreciate the character they have demonstrated can have powerful results.

It is ironic that the appropriate granting of recognition is so often neglected, for it costs little. Usually the only expense is the effort on the part of the leader to arrange a way to become aware of the efforts and accomplishments of those being led.

> "The sweetest of all sounds is praise."
> Xenophon

5) An Effective Leader Equips Subordinates

Seminar participants say that they are more likely to willingly follow a leader who provides them whatever is needed to help them do their jobs. It is difficult and sometimes impossible to follow leaders who neglect this important issue. Ironically, I have found that this is one of the most neglected responsibilities of those in authority. The concept mentioned earlier, *servant leadership,* also applies here. True leaders accept the role of providing their followers with everything possible to facilitate the job.

As a chief officer in the Los Angeles Police Department it came to my attention that a detective division was being inundated with homicide investigations. I wanted to help them cope with their increasing workload, but I made a simple error—I decided how I would help them without getting their input.

Homicide investigations usually involve lengthy and complex reports. The whole investigation must be documented. Statements of witnesses, descriptions of crime scenes, and the analysis of evidence are just a few of the many necessary reports. Having had experience as a detective, I recalled the many hours of work I had to devote to preparing reports. I decided that dictation equipment would shorten this time. I secured sufficient dictating equipment and clerical help, then asked the detectives to begin using the devices and cease handwriting their reports.

A few days later I stopped by to check on the impact of my decision. I observed one detective reading from his *handwritten* report into one of the new dictating devices. I checked a couple of other detectives and learned that I unwittingly had increased the reporting time in most cases. I had not considered the fact that dictating is a skill that must be taught and/or developed.

Equipping people involves a broad spectrum of support. Providing training, education, mentoring, and technical equipment are just a few examples of this successful leadership behavior. Tom Janes knew I had far less experience than those I was leading, so he arranged for me to get special training at the Northwestern University Traffic Institute. The course he wanted me to take lasted ten months. Tom arranged for me to get a scholarship and also permitted me to take my whole family with me to Chicago where I was studying.

6) An Effective Leader Removes Barriers

In my opinion, few leaders purposely create obstructions that hinder their followers. Conversely, most are willing to remove unnecessary barriers. Still, one of the most common complaints of people being led is the number of problems created or ignored by their leaders. In large bureaucracies, the problems are often called *administrative hoops* that workers must jump through. These "hoops" are usually set up to prevent misconduct, abuse of power, fiscal irresponsibility, or to ensure a standard of performance. Redundant paperwork is a common manifestation of these problems.

At one time, it was necessary for officers in the LAPD to prepare four separate reports to document the arrest of a person driving under the influence of alcohol (DUI). Many officers viewed these reports as needless, redundant hoops. Some officers actually avoided making DUI arrests due to these complications. Management did not purposely create these reports to make the job difficult. Each report resulted from some important mandate, but the end result was still a hindrance.

Since DUI violations account for over half of the nation's traffic deaths, Captain Tom Janes worked hard to remove barriers that hampered enforcement activities. He had the four separate reports consolidated into one document that still met management objectives. Also, a mobile jail unit was employed to facilitate the booking of arrestees. The result was a dramatic increase in enforcement activities and the reduction of traffic collisions involving under-the-influence drivers.

Besides burdensome regulations, there are other barriers to good work. One example is failure to appropriately delegate. This type of barrier can be manifested as requirements to obtain permission prior to taking action. One way to lower or eliminate barriers of this nature is to emphasize principles, secure commitment to the principles, delegate authority, and then hold followers accountable. This will be addressed further in chapter 12 on Principle-Based Leadership.

Support/staff units or individuals often unwittingly erect barriers. Their role of assisting people doing the primary job can end up doing the opposite. Often the problem here is that systems intended to provide information, equipment, or services for workers are designed by staff personnel for their own convenience.

As a chief officer, I had a policy of occasionally working a shift with a patrol officer or detective. I found that keeping current with the actual performance of the job at the operating level was essential for me as a policy decision maker. On each of these occasions, I learned something important about the changing job of street police officers. Coincidentally, I also had the opportunity to provide insights to my partner without the filtering of several layers of supervision.

On one of these experiences, I worked with a salty street cop. As we left the roll-call assembly and loaded our equipment into the patrol car, he asked, "Do you want to drive or write?"

I told him that when people came into my office, I was in charge. "However, since we're working in your 'office,' you're in charge. I'll be your junior partner."

"Good!" he responded. "You do the paperwork then. I'll drive."

I soon learned that *paperwork* included working the squad car computer. The first-generation computers that we had installed were definitely not user friendly. Receiving information from the dispatcher and automated systems was not a problem, but inputting information was. Our first call involved the investigation of a simple assault. A dispute had turned into a fight and the loser registered a complaint. I took a misdemeanor battery report that would later be submitted to the prosecutor's office.

Back in the patrol car, I punched the *clear* button on the computer, indicating we were available for another call. The computer asked me for a *dispo* (disposition) on our last call. My senior partner snickered as I tried to work the computer using plain English. Finally, he handed me a small booklet that he kept in one of his uniform shirt pockets. "Look in here and you'll get the numerical code for *crime report*. The computer will accept the code. It won't accept something simple like English."

As I discovered that night, the automated systems people programmed made it simple for *them* to gather data. But their system made it extremely hard for street cops to do their job. The next day I issued directives to re-program the computers to do what they were supposed to do—help the men and women on the street do their jobs.

7) An Effective Leader Is Consistent
Seminar participants registered a strong consensus on this dimension of leadership. Some of them described this trait as "Not saying one thing today and then taking the opposite position tomorrow." Others described good leaders as predictable. Leaders are predictable when they are consistent. Regardless of the words used to explain their opinion, agreement on the value of this characteristic was obvious.

People like to follow someone who remains solid rather than wishy-washy on issues. This is particularly important when the leader is not present or immediately available to grant permission or give authority to his or her followers. If the leader is consistent, the followers may choose to take action based upon their knowledge of the leader's past decisions. In other words, the leader's predictability empowers the followers to make decisions in his or her absence.

Consistency also reduces the fear of being second guessed or subjected to "Monday morning quarterbacking." Inconsistency breeds insecurity. Decision-makers often refuse to make needed decisions because they fear criticism by their leader. When they see a great deal of waffling or changing of positions on issues by leadership, they become unwilling to take the risk of being wrong. Security may be established or restored by a leader that is willing to take strong, clear positions on matters of policy and principle.

One weekend day, Sergeant Don Murphy (a fictitious name) showed up for work with bloodshot eyes and alcohol on his breath. As he walked past Jim Davin, a former Marine sitting at the reception desk, I saw Jim roll his eyes. He noticed it too. Don had been drinking.

Don had a history of alcohol abuse. We had put him on the day watch, required him to enroll in a treatment program, and watched him carefully. He had been doing great for several months. Now, here he was, presenting a tough problem for me. I was a new lieutenant, assigned as the day watch commander at AID (Accident Investigation Division). The "Skipper," Tom Janes, was out of town and not available for advice. Yet, I did not have to give it much thought to know what to do. Janes was consistent on this issue. He had discussed the principle behind our policy regarding unusual enforcement situations. I could almost hear him saying the words, "Collect the evidence." Regardless of who the person is—a VIP, a U. S. senator, someone with diplomatic immunity, or a noncriminal employee violation. "Collect the evidence, preserve the facts."

Don was not intoxicated. He was not violating the law. But he was certainly violating our personnel policies. I could not allow him to work with the odor of alcohol on his breath. I had several alternatives on how to handle this problem. One thing was certain. If I clearly established all of the facts regarding this situation, things could be repaired. That is exactly what I did.

To avoid embarrassing the sergeant, I had Jim Davin bring a breath-testing device into the vacant captain's office. Then, in the privacy of the office, I ordered Don to give a breath sample for analysis. I asked him all of the relevant questions. Then I called in another sergeant to sit in for me while I drove Don home.

Later, when I presented the paperwork on this incident to Captain Janes, he reinforced what I had done in establishing the facts. I could have taken another course of action rather than take him home. For example, I could have had the sergeant stay in the station until all indications of his alcohol consumption were dissipated. But now that all of the facts were established, appropriate disciplinary action could be taken.

8) An Effective Leader Displays Good Judgment

People like to follow someone who makes decisions that prove wise and correct most of the time. Good judgment was identified as a behavior that flows from a certain attitude or approach to life. Seminar participants have indicated that although good judgment is difficult to quantify or define, "you know it when you see it." They also recognized that this trait could be developed through experience. Although they also recognized that an individual might have a wealth of experience and yet lack good judgment.

No one likes to follow a "loser." People like to follow someone who establishes a track record of making good decisions. People like to be on a winning team. They enjoy being a part of a successful enterprise. Leaders who exhibit wisdom and insight through their decisions are admired and respected, even if they are not liked. Of course, no one is perfect and occasional errors of good faith are usually tolerated. This is especially true when the error is admitted and corrected, if possible.

Seminar participants differentiated good judgment from knowledge. They recognized that a person might lack knowledge about a specific subject and yet make wise decisions in that field or discipline. Often, relying on the expertise of others accomplishes this.

This was important for me to learn when I was in the Accident Investigation Division. Having little traffic experience, I simply had to rely on my staff who had more knowledge and experience. Captain Tom Janes reminded me on several occasions that it is easy to lead a team when you are the expert. The challenge is leading when your staff knows more than you do.

Chief William H. Parker, recognized by many as one of the great police chiefs of our time, is a good example of this concept. When Parker began leading the amazing transformation of the Los Angeles Police Department, he had limited police experience. He had strong expertise in traffic enforcement. He was a graduate of Northwestern University's Traffic Institute. He worked as a traffic enforcement officer, but his experience in other aspects of police work was somewhat limited. Nevertheless, he pulled off a major change of a large bureaucracy in a relatively short period of time. He changed a second-rate, corrupt police department into an efficient, professional, and well-respected agency. Even his detractors admired his savvy. What was Parker's secret? In my opinion, he developed good judgment by recognizing his own strengths *and weaknesses*. He led by explaining broad principles to his followers and then depended heavily on their expertise to tend to the details.

> *"The man who knows right from wrong
> and has good judgment and common sense
> is happier than the man who is immensely rich."*
> The Book of Proverbs –circa 935 BC [6]

9) An Effective Leader Is Fair

Few issues can undermine and destroy a leader's effectiveness more profoundly than a perception of a lack of objectivity, favoritism, or unfairness. Conversely, followers will accept many unpopular decisions and mandates from authority as long as they are perceived as fair.

Fairness means that people are assigned, promoted, and rewarded on the basis of some measure of objectivity. A fair boss makes personnel decisions based upon performance rather than friendship. When the CEO's golfing partners are quickly promoted in spite of their well-known inadequacy, the general morale of the organization suffers.

People enjoy working in an environment when it is commonly known that discipline is consistent, rewards are based upon superior performance, and everyone has a chance to realize their dreams.

Shortly after my thirty-sixth birthday, I was promoted to the rank of captain. In preparation for this awesome responsibility of leading over three hundred men and women in a high-risk profession, I was sent to our command school. One of the significant portions of the curriculum focused on discipline. I would be responsible for directing the investigations of all charges of misconduct lodged against the officers of my command and recommending appropriate disciplinary action to the chief of police. The commander in charge of Internal Affairs Division spent several hours explaining the whole disciplinary process to all of us in the class. He devoted much of his time to the issue of fairness. I will never forget his words explaining the important issue of balancing the interests of the concerned officer and the perception of the entire Department. The central point of his remarks addressed this important factor of fairness.

---

[6] The New American Standard Bible, (La Habra: Foundation Press, 1960) Proverbs 3:13–15

10) An Effective Leader Emphasizes Principles—Not Merely Rules

This trait was defined with more diversity of terms than all of the rest combined. Some groups stated they wanted a boss who explained the reasons behind a direction given. Others said they appreciated a leader who gave clear but broad policy guidance, but left some room for them to make specific application based upon individual circumstances. Some groups described leaders who tell them *what* they want done, but allow them to determine how to do it. An emphasis of principle seems to address all of the responses falling in this group. Principle explains the *why.* Principle addresses the broad issues. Principle offers a foundation for individual application.

Leaders who talk in terms of principles offer their followers a view into their minds. Rather than treating the followers like robots who are simply expected to follow orders, they treat them as peers. The very discussion of principles assumes that the listeners are capable of conceptualizing at that level of thought. In a very real sense they are brought in on the motives, purposes, values, and ethics of the leader.

A discussion of principles also allows the leader to grant more power to those being led. If they can communicate the principles with sufficient conviction to obtain commitment to them, the details of how to translate them into strategies, procedures, and actions can and should be delegated.

Tom Janes knew I had some aptitude with math. He exploited my interest and ability in this area in a positive sense. First, he sat me down and explained what we were trying to achieve as an important division of the LAPD. He discussed the principle of specialization. Then he applied the principle to our operation. He explained the advantages of having our specially trained officers (rather than general patrol officers) investigate the traffic accidents occurring in our city. That meant we had to deploy our officers efficiently according to the uneven frequencies of occurrences. That was a challenge. But once I understood the principle involved and our objective based on that principle, I threw myself into the difficult task of developing a formula for ensuring that officers were deployed according to projected needs. I actually enjoyed the task he gave me.

Leadership: The Power of Character

People like to follow leaders who emphasize principles because they want to be part of the team. They want the agenda to be open rather than hidden. They want to contribute their expertise, skills, and insight to the enterprise. They want to be valued as colleagues. In order to do this, they must see the goal, understand the mission; they must share the dream. Talking principles makes these things happen.

11) An Effective Leader Is Champion of Followers
Respondents described a good leader as one who is willing to fight for his or her followers. They indicated they wanted their leader to look out for their interests, protect their rights, and be an insulator to interfering pressure or heat. Followers must often operate in an environment that they cannot control. By environment I refer to the broad spectrum of factors that make up their operational setting, such as the physical, political, social, economic, and ethical aspects of the arena within which they operate. They want their leader to care about these important influences in their lives. They want a champion to defend them, support their cause, and take action to make their environment better.

Those of us working AID were frustrated. Our prosecutions of people driving under the influence of alcohol were dramatically up. We realized that of the nearly one thousand people a week dying in traffic accidents nationwide, over half were the result of combining alcohol consumption with driving. Yet, the courts continued to be soft on these deadly offenders. And to make matters worse, the city attorney's office resisted prosecuting those with "low BA's" (blood alcohol levels between .10–.12%). The law at that time presumed that anything over .10% was under the influence. In most states, the level in 2002 was .08%.

Captain Tom Janes demonstrated this concept of being a champion of his followers. He went to several auto insurance companies and secured funding. Then he invited the prosecutors and judges to a special dinner at the police academy. Prior to dinner, he had several volunteers from both groups begin drinking alcoholic beverages. He asked them to volunteer to submit to a breath test analysis <u>when they felt they were impaired and should not drive</u>. Several of us were there to administer field sobriety tests to the volunteers in front of their

36

Leadership: The Power of Character

peers. All of the volunteers *failed* the tests and recognized that they should not drive. Then the big surprise! After testing their blood alcohol content, the highest level was .07%.

The "contestants" were all driven home. Everyone in attendance was profoundly impacted. The problem of overly tolerant prosecutors and judges was resolved. Tom Janes was our champion.

Often the leader is the only one who has the power or influence to make a difference. Followers are often victimized by customers, high-ranking officers within the organization, or leaders of associate organizations when their leader is not willing to assume the role of champion of his or her followers. A wise leader recognizes the importance of this function and accepts the challenge.

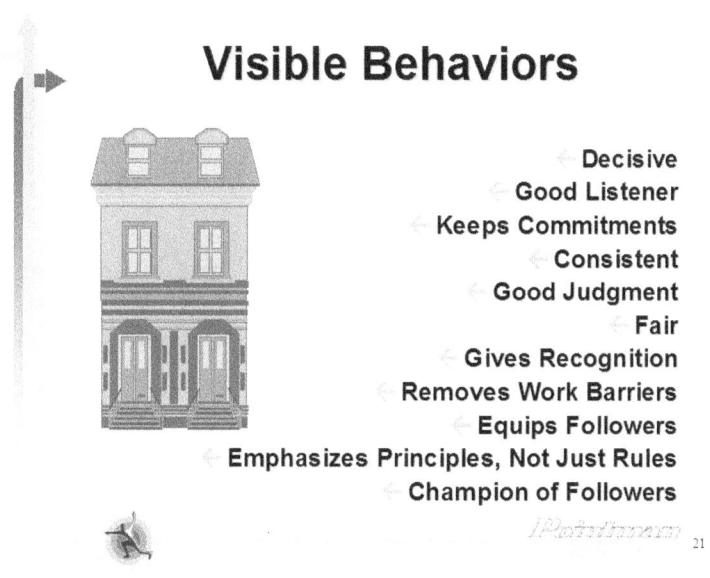

Figure 1

Summary

There is amazing agreement about the behaviors that support effective leadership. While these behaviors make effective leaders, for most people, these behaviors do not come naturally. They can be learned and practiced, but often they will not hold up under pressure. In our seminars, we present the above PowerPoint presentation. The house is representative of the behavior than can be observed. But what cannot be readily seen (the foundation) holds the key to the stability of the house. . So how does a leader develop a foundational character so that these behaviors become natural? Answering that question is the purpose of the next few chapters.

Plan for Success
1. Identify the behaviors you practice regularly as a leader.
2. Identify the behaviors that are neglected in your leadership style.
3. Plan a strategy to focus attention on the behaviors you believe will make you more effective.
4. Ask your followers to identify behaviors where you can improve.

Chapter 4
The Necessity of Foundation

While presenting our seminar in Saratov, Russia, a humorous event took place. We had just presented the behaviors identified in the previous chapter. Then I asked the participants to indicate how many leaders they knew who consistently applied those behaviors. Suddenly, I realized I had put them in an awkward position. Behind me on the platform sat several of the top leaders of Russia, including the Deputy Minister of Justice. I felt they would be compelled to hold up at least three fingers to keep in the good graces of their superiors. So, I tried to relieve them of the stress I had placed on them.

I said: *"Please eliminate from your consideration your leaders on the platform."* I waited as my translator explained my instructions to the participants. Suddenly, one of the other translators jumped to his feet (translation work is so demanding we always hire more than one). He shouted: "Nyet, Nyet," meaning "No, No." He then began speaking urgently in the Russian language, apparently about something of importance.

One of the Generals on the platform had risen to his feet and appeared angry. Many of those in the room began speaking rapidly to one another. Then someone began laughing. Then they all began laughing. I wondered what had just occurred.

One of the translators approached me, and in English explained what had transpired. The first translator had mistakenly interpreted my instructions. He had spoken in Russian: *"General Vernon says you should annihilate your leaders on the platform!"* No wonder the three men on the platform reacted negatively to my statement. The second translator to speak had corrected my instructions. Fortunately, the three leaders saw the humor of what had just happened. I was spared a long-term "vacation" in one of the colonies in Siberia.

But the most significant insight to come from that event was yet to follow. Once the correction was made and the participants reacted to my true intentions, the results were the same as I have experience in most settings. As they responded to my request to indicate how many leaders they knew who consistently applied the desired behaviors, many participants began shaking their heads indicating "No." Others said words in Russian that my interpreter explained meant "no one." Two or three held up one finger, indicating just one. This reaction is consistent with the reaction we have experienced in all of our seminars.

We have found that the eleven *behaviors* just enumerated in the previous chapter are those most commonly described as desirable in leaders. The collection of this information has taken place in a variety of cultural, socio/economic and organizational settings, including the United States of America. Yet, the content of the input has been remarkably consistent.

At the same time, another consistent pattern has emerged. Participants in our seminars have indicated another strong consensus. When asked how many "leaders" they have observed who consistently demonstrate this behavior, a vast majority records "none." Few record one or two. This is a strange paradox. There is strong agreement on the concepts of leadership with little indication of the practice of those concepts.

The consensus on effective leadership behavior is not surprising or revealing. Most or all of these behaviors are well documented in the many books available on the topics of leadership, management or supervision. The curious issue is their lack of application. If effective leadership behavior is clearly identified, why is it rarely practiced with consistency?

Big Consensus / Little Application

To me it seems ironic that although there is much agreement on what type of behavior patterns lead to effective leadership, there is also a strong consensus that few people consistently exhibit those behaviors. Why is this so? It would seem that if we know the pattern for leadership success, more of us would practice it. Yet this does not seem to be the case. There is a gap between what we know is effective leadership behavior and the actual practice of that behavior.

In figure 1, page 35, I have illustrated the desirable leadership behaviors as the structural components of a building. I have a two-fold purpose of using a building as an illustration of effective leadership. First, effective leadership is the result of a combination of behavioral components that make up the whole of a successful package. Similarly, a building is made up of a number of structural components. Secondly, effective leadership behaviors are recognizable. They can be observed and measured. Once again the components of a building can be observed and measured.

Foundation Lacking

Much of the attention of leadership education and training has been directed toward these observable behaviors. This is appropriate and necessary; but it does not go far enough. If a building is to survive the elements, if it is to last through the stress of weather and earthquakes, then the unseen foundation is all-important. Similarly, if an observable effective leadership style is to survive, it too must be supported by a firm foundation of ethics or character. Like the foundation of a building, these attributes may be difficult to observe and evaluate; but they are just as important and related to behavior as a solid foundation is to a stable structure.

San Francisco suffered an earthquake registering 7.2 on the Richter Scale in 1989. Over fifty people lost their lives in this disaster. Most of the deaths were a result of the collapse of a double layer freeway. In other parts of the world, when an earthquake of that magnitude hits a similarly populated area, often hundreds or thousands of lives are lost. Why the disparity? The difference is in construction; specifically in the design and construction of the **foundation** of the buildings involved.

Similarly, the consistent application of effective leadership behavior is dependent upon the presence or lack of foundational character traits. A person's behavior is related directly to his/her core beliefs or ethics. Therefore if one is interested in consistently demonstrating certain desirable behavior, their ethics, absolutes or character traits must be considered.

Ethic is defined as:

> *The discipline (implying actions) dealing with what is good and bad and with moral duty and obligation; a set of moral principles or values.* [7]

In the context of our considerations, it will become apparent how commitment to a set of moral principles will have profound effect on a leader's capability to maintain the desired behavior.

I have acted as a consultant to various governmental and private organizations. On some of these occasions the group or individual is attempting to diagnose a problem in order to implement a solution. On one occasion several of the leaders of a city were very unhappy with the performance of their police chief. They wanted to either get rid of him or in some other way solve what they perceived to be a serious problem. They explained to me that the morale of the officers was low. Consequently, their performance had decreased profoundly. Many officers were retiring, resigning and/or moving to other law enforcement agencies.

I began my analysis by asking a number of key questions about the actions of the Chief. Their answers to my questions revealed that the Chief seemed well versed in techniques of leadership and management. His actions and decisions they described were, in most cases, sound. He was apparently demonstrating most of the eleven behaviors discussed in Chapter Two of this book.

Eventually, I pointed out to them that according to their own description of the Chief and his actions, he seemed to be in compliance with accepted professional standards. Additionally, I told them that his recent decisions

---

[7] <u>Webster's 7th New Collegiate Dictionary;</u> (G & C. Merriam Company 1965)

reflected good judgment. Then the real issues began to emerge. "But he doesn't care," one of them almost shouted. Over the next few minutes the group quickly focused on another dimension of the Chief – his *character*. I soon discovered they were not so much concerned about the chief's decisions or actions. Rather they were concerned about the way in which he interacted with people. They were concerned about what they thought were his motives, ethics and attitudes. They perceived him to be arrogant, uncaring and negative.

This and many other similar experiences have caused me to understand that being educated in the behaviors of leadership is not enough. Effective leadership is about character. The motives, convictions and attitudes of the leaders are indeed important.

Falling Back to Plan B

Most of us have been exposed to an assessment of our leadership style through the application of a self-test scale. The exercise involves responding to a number of questions. Based upon one's response to these questions a profile of leadership behavior is developed. Usually it is suggested that under normal circumstances an individual uses one leadership style; but when put under pressure or stress will change quickly to a "Plan B" style of behavior. The "Plan B" adaptation is dysfunctional to effective leadership. I can identify with these phenomena.

In today's real world, it is possible to experience stress more often than the "fair weather" times. Consequently, it is typical to be in the dysfunctional "Plan B" mode much of the time.

A fairly new captain arranged for a career counseling appointment with me. He wanted to change assignments from commanding one of our support divisions to one of our eighteen field divisions. Commanding one of our field divisions of over three hundred line officers is desirable by commanders seeking action and interested in future promotions.

I knew the Captain was intelligent and resourceful. He had a master's degree. He had done well on the promotional examinations. He had a good grasp of the policies of the organization. In short, he was well qualified as far as his knowledge and skills. He did have a major problem. He was easily influenced by the "pressure to please." When this pressure came to bear which was often, he abandoned the behaviors he had been taught. For example, he gave his superiors information he knew they would want to hear and censor out the "bad news" they actually needed to hear. With subordinates, he would choose behavior intended to secure popularity, unknowingly at the expense of respect.

I explained to him that in my opinion he often shifted to his less effective "Plan B" of leadership. I told him that it appeared to me that he was more interested in getting the acceptance and approval of people rather than having a firm commitment to a set of beliefs or convictions. The conversation was very direct. His eyes became moist when I told him the truth about his image. I concluded by explaining to him the action he had to take in order to overcome this deficiency. Then I promised him I would watch him carefully over the next few months, and if sufficient progress were made in his character development, would transfer him to a line command.

This was a classic case of one knowing a lot about the right behaviors and often practicing it, but reverting to a less effective set of behaviors due to a lack of character foundation. The good news is that the Captain took significant action. He shifted his focus to the foundation. The result was that he became more consistent in his "Plan A" style of behavior. Eventually he was moved to the command he sought, proved himself in it and was later promoted.

I am suggesting that this negative adaptation does not have to occur. At least it can be greatly retarded if there is a firm foundation for the desirable leadership style. I strongly believe that focusing attention on ethics can help build a firm foundation for effective leadership behavior. It is my opinion that we have mistakenly overlooked the most important element in one's behavior and that is one's belief system. The good news is that when one refocuses his/her attention to the "foundation," their good leadership behavior can become more consistent.

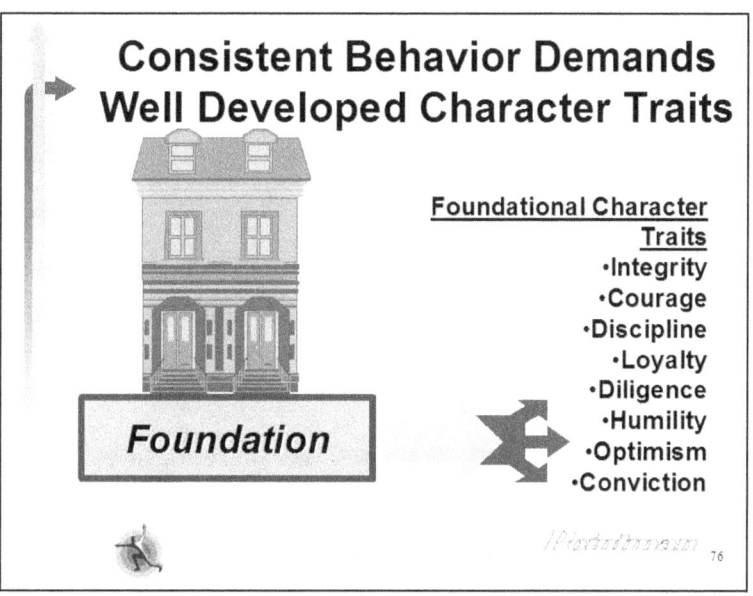

Figure 2

Many sound well-engineered buildings have a foundation of concrete. Concrete is composed of several components mixed in the appropriate ratios. Cement, sand, rock or gravel, water and reinforcing steel are the most common elements. Each of them by themselves will be insufficient for a strong foundation. When mixed together, they form a very firm and strong composite. The character of a leader is similar. It is composed of several elements. I am suggesting that a composite of the ethics or character traits outlined in Figure 2 can form the foundation for consistent effective leadership behavior.

As in the case of concrete, individual components will be insufficient. Integrity, courage and conviction without humility can result in someone who is despised as a "know it all." It is my opinion that all eight must be pursued.

Leadership: The Power of Character

Summary

The traditional approach to discussing leadership often focuses on **behavior**. There is a strong consensus on the types of behavior that lead to effective and powerful leadership. Information about effective leadership behavior has been widely disseminated during the latter part of the 20th century. Yet at the same time there seems to be a leadership vacuum. It is my opinion that we have neglected to properly address the character issue involved in consistent leadership behavior.

Our behavior is invariably linked to our core beliefs, values and ethics. Yet we have unwittingly assumed we can build a beautiful "structure" of leadership behavior without addressing the foundation of such a structure.

Character is related to behavior.

In my opinion, true leadership as we have defined it is more related to character than a person's technical skills. In other words, the consistent application of the behavior patterns that are widely accepted as necessary to leadership must be supported by character that includes several essential ethics.

In Part II we will outline eight basic character traits, or ethics, mandatory for leadership (Figure 2). They will be presented from a utilitarian rather than a moralistic viewpoint.

Plan for Success:
1. Examine the behaviors listed on Figure 1 and compare them to the foundational ethics or character traits listed on Figure 2
2. Which Character traits may relate to the leadership behaviors you have selected to focus upon?
3. What type of stress may cause you to revert to "Plan B?"

Part II
Eight Core Character Traits

Chapter 5
<u>Integrity</u>

I believe the most important ethic or character trait that forms the foundation for sustained, effective leadership behavior is integrity (Figure 2, page 38). The word integrity comes from the root ***integer*** meaning whole or undivided. In mathematics, it is the opposite of a fraction. Integrity is defined as:

An unimpaired condition; soundness; adherence to a code of moral, artistic, or other values; the state of being complete or undivided. [8]

Therefore someone with integrity is whole rather than divided. A person of integrity performs actions that match his/her stated beliefs or values. Someone with integrity is **one** *person* rather than several personalities based upon the present circumstance. Integrity is the opposite of duplicity. Duplicity is that trait of being double minded (more than one) or one of deception. In colloquial language we speak of a person with an integrity deficit as being "two faced." Integrity means therefore someone who is truthful; someone who keeps his/her word or promise; someone who is authentic and therefore trustworthy.

A significant integrity problem has emerged in the United States of America. It is now acceptable to make a "technically accurate" statement with a clear intent to deceive. Many do not consider this behavior wrong. For example, an employee asks his/her boss about a rumor that he/she is being moved to a less desirable assignment. The decision was supposedly made at a management meeting on Wednesday. The boss was at a meeting on Tuesday

---

[8] <u>Webster's 7th New Collegiate Dictionary</u>; (G & C. Merriam Company 1965)

where indeed that decision was made. The boss for whatever reason does not want to reveal the decision yet. The boss states: "No, no. Don't worry about that rumor. There was no such meeting on Wednesday." The answer is technically correct, but clearly is an attempt to deceive. If the boss has a legitimate reason for not yet disclosing the decision (i.e. it may not be final), the more appropriate answer would be: "It would not be appropriate for me to talk about discussions in our last management meeting at this point." Leaders who make "technically accurate" statements with intent to deceive will be looked upon as not trustworthy. Their trust factor will erode. Such a person may justify his/her statements in their own mind; but their followers will see the deception for what it is – **a lie**.

Predictability

Integrity makes someone predictable. I mean a helpful kind of predictability. I am talking about the kind of predictability that gives followers guidance when the leader is not present or available. This kind of predictability occurs when someone has a strong set of convictions (Chapter 11) and has the integrity to "stick" to them.

I presented this seminar to a group of leaders in a South American country. A leader objected to being "predictable." When I asked him to explain his objection to this trait he gave an answer that helped me understand that he was referring to a different kind of predictability. He explained that he had a problem with some of his followers abusing alcohol while performing their duties. He stated it became necessary for him to observe, unannounced, their behavior in order to stop this abuse. He did not want his on-site inspections to become predictable. I agreed with him.

His objection allowed me to clarify the type of predictability that I am promoting. I am not advocating predictability of a leader's methods of holding people accountable. I am advocating being predictable about what principles one believes and acts out. One such principle in this case could be that providing professional service demands sobriety, unhampered by intoxication. In this case one would want to be predictable about not tolerating drinking alcohol while performing government service.

When a leader is known for having strong beliefs and most importantly *living* by them, he or she becomes predictable in the sense of providing guidance. People have confidence in following someone who is consistent in this regard. This consistency allows the followers to predict how the leader would respond to a given situation even when the leader is not present and unavailable for counsel. This predictability gives the followers the confidence to make the correct decision on their own.

The Cardinal Factor

Integrity is basic to **sustained** effective leadership. It is a threshold ("make or break") issue. One can lack integrity and demonstrate effective leadership behavior for a period of time. But eventually his/her lack of integrity will become exposed. At that point effective leadership begins to diminish.

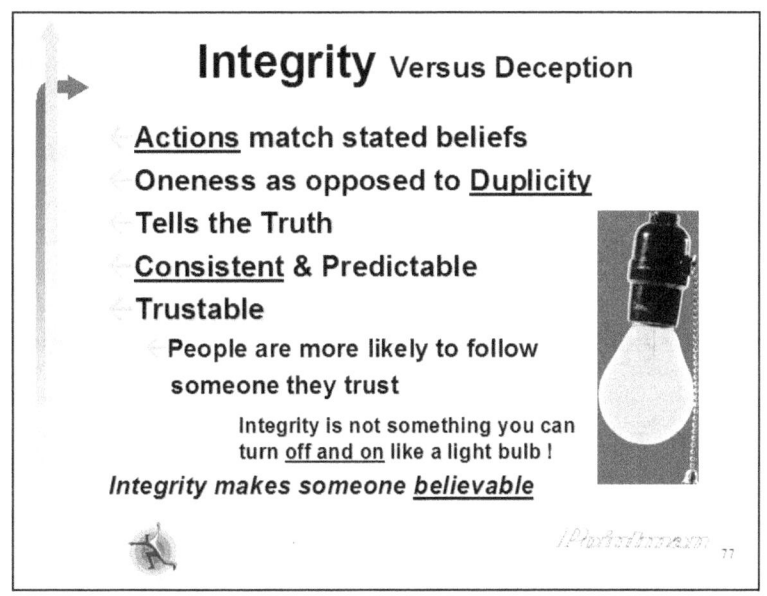

Figure 3

Peter Drucker describes integrity as the most critical issue qualifying one for leadership.

> ". . . it is character through which leadership is exercised; it is character that sets the example and is imitated."
> ". . . it is not something one can fool people about. The men with whom a man works, and especially his subordinates, know in a few weeks whether he has **integrity** or not. They may forgive a man a great deal: incompetence, ignorance, insecurity, or bad manners. But they will not forgive his lack of integrity. Nor will they forgive higher management for choosing him." [9]

This basic truth has been recognized for centuries. An ancient proverb states: *"The man who walks in integrity walks securely; the man who walks the crooked path will eventually be exposed."* The Book of Proverbs 18 Circa 935 B.C.[10]

You Will be Exposed

I have found that the size of the group being led has a relationship to the time it takes for the result of a lack of integrity to have an effect. For example, in a small company of 35 employees a lack of integrity by the CEO will have an obvious negative impact in a relative short time of weeks or months. In the case of a very large organization such as The United States of America, the consequences of an integrity deficit in its leadership may take years to surface.

Integrity is basic to leadership for a very important reason. Leadership requires trust. In a sense, those being led are granting the leader control over their lives, at least control over that portion of their lives the leader is trying to influence. They are submitting to the influence of the leader. In order to do that

---

[9] Drucker, *Management: tasks, responsibilities, practices.* (Harper & Roe, NY 1973) p 462

[10] The New American Standard Bible: (Foundation Press, La Habra, CA. 1960) Proverbs 10:18

there must be a strong element of trust. When trust is eroded, influence begins to wane.

Should I Shoot?

Early in my career I worked with an amazing training officer, Fernando "Nick" Najera. "Nick" had won a Silver Star at Bastogne, Belgium, while serving with the 101st Airborne in WW II. He had joined the Los Angeles Police Department soon after mustering out of the army. When I joined the police department in 1954, he already had eight years of street police work experience under his belt.

Nick was a great role model for a rookie cop. He had developed a good measure of "street savvy," without becoming overly cynical or losing his enthusiasm for the job. He knew his business and he enjoyed it. I was soon "infected" by his love for police work. But that was not the most significant part of Nick. Above and beyond everything else, Nick had integrity. If Nick made promises, he kept them. If he said something was so, it was. He told the truth, even if it meant losing a case. In short, Nick was trustable. During those first few years on the street, my life was in his hands on many occasions. He always came through. Even if it meant putting his own life on the line.

One afternoon we "rolled" on a rape case. We were working a "plain clothes" assignment providing preliminary follow-up on felony cases. When we arrived on the scene, uniformed officers in a black and white patrol car were already there. A woman had been viciously attacked and raped. Her assailant had used a pistol to club her into submission. He had been brutal. Her nose was broken, teeth knocked out and jaw fractured.

The uniformed officers at the scene gave us a description of the suspect written on the back of an "F.I." (Field Interview) card. They explained that he left on foot shortly before their arrival, pointing in the direction of his flight. They told us they would stay with the victim until the ambulance arrived. We jumped in our car and took off in pursuit while broadcasting the information to other units in the area.

Leadership: The Power of Character

Although we were in a plain vehicle, it was no secret as to who we were. We were driving a new Ford, four-door sedan. The car was the basic "plain wrap" model, with three aerials and two big guys inside with shades looking around. As we followed his trail, people in the neighborhood were expecting us and pointed in the direction of his flight. At almost every corner there was someone pointing.

The trail led us to The Lincoln Heights Auto Court. We had been here before. It was a run-down combination trailer park and collection of small two room cabins; and a hangout for undesirables. We went to the manager's office and showed her the description of the suspect. She explained that she had two men who fit the description. One was in cabin #2; the other up on the hill in #38. We chose #2 to try first. Nick told me I was "up", meaning I would go to the front door. He would cover the rear door.

It was a small two room shingled cabin with a small wooden porch. The outside front door was open. The boards squeaked as I stepped up on the porch. I could see the silhouette of a man step into the internal doorway between the kitchenette and the combination living room/bedroom. I jerked the locked screen door open, stepping into the living room. I had pulled my six-inch, .38 police special caliber, colt revolver from my shoulder holster and was pointing it at him. He fit the description. I held my badge in my left hand and shouted: "Police Officers - - Freeze!"

I could see all of his body except the most important part -- his hands. His arms were outstretched in what appeared to be a two handed shooting position, pointing toward the back door where my partner had deployed. I could not see his hands. They were out of my view behind the wall next to the doorway. Rather than comply with my command, he moved suddenly toward the direction of his hands. Now, I could only see one of his feet and a portion of the leg.

I crouched low in combat shooting position so as to form a smaller target. I dropped my badge and now held my gun with both hands. I began applying pressure to the trigger. *Remember squeeze slowly. Don't jerk the gun off the target. His* body began to reappear in the doorway. All my senses told me, "*He's got the gun. He's going to shoot*!"

Suddenly, Nick shouted: "Hold it Bob!"

He had entered the small cabin through the back door and was in the same room as the suspect. All of my instincts and training told me to shoot. The man's body was moving into a position where he could shoot me. Why did he ignore my command to "Freeze?" Why did he move quickly to get something when I had my gun pointing at him? It didn't make sense. Why was Nick telling me not to shoot?

It became a matter of trust. All of my experience with Nick overwhelmed my own perceptions. I knew I could trust him. He had integrity. He had earned my trust. I did not understand the "Why"; but in that instant of time, I decided to follow his leadership. Thank God I did. The man was not the assailant we were after. He was not armed.

After the adrenaline rush was over, here is the story that emerged. The man in the cabin was peeling potatoes at the small sink in the kitchen. He heard someone step on his porch and stepped backward into the doorway to see who was there. He had a partially peeled potato in his hand and tried to continue holding it over the sink. A stranger jerked the screen door open and pointed a gun at him shouting, "Police Officers, . . . Freeze!" He was frightened. He flinched. The slippery potato shot out of his hands like a bar of soap. In reflex action, he went after it. It all made sense once I understood all of the facts. By the way, we arrested our suspect in # 38, without any resistance or problems.

The Critical Connection

The point of this story is to illustrate the nexus or connection between trust and leadership. Although this incident is a little more dramatic than most leadership situations, it does reveal an important principle. For people to follow a leader when the concerned facts are limited, there must be trust. Add to that thought the fact that in most cases involving leadership, all of the particulars are not available to those being led.

Every phase of leadership involves trust. There must be trust that the leader is leading in the right direction. There must be trust that he/she will support the actions of the followers as long as they operate within the agreed upon parameters; trust that he/she will keep commitments. There must be trust in his/her judgment; trust that the leader provides accurate information. And perhaps most importantly, trust that his/her motives are not self centered but rather altruistic – with the interests of the team in first place. In short, the leader must be trustable

Integrity breeds trust. People tend to believe in someone with integrity. People of duplicity should be doubted and questioned. There is understandably little or no trust of a person who lies, breaks promises or demonstrates a pattern of weak character.

Peter Drucker believes a lack of integrity is corrosive:

". . . But if he (leader) lacks in character and integrity -- no matter how knowledgeable, how brilliant, how successful-- he destroys. He destroys people, the most valuable resource of the enterprise. He destroys spirit. And he destroys performance." [11]

"On or Off?"

Integrity is not like a light bulb. It cannot be turned off and on. You either have it or you don't. You cannot practice duplicity in your private life and expect to be trusted in your public or professional life. If one demonstrates a lack of integrity in his/her personal life, it is reasonable to assume that fact will eventually become known at work. This will reveal a breech in the "soundness" of the character. It will illustrate an impairment that causes doubt. If one departs from a state of integrity (turns off the switch), others will justifiably wonder when next the switch will be moved. Will the "switch" be moved at the work place? How is one to know if the "switch" is on or off?

The ancient philosopher, Solomon, compared a reputation of integrity to a treasure of gold or silver. *"A good name is to be more desired than great riches,*

---

[11] Drucker, *Management: tasks, responsibilities, practices*. (Harper & Roe, NY 1973) p462

Favor is better than silver and gold." [12] I believe he had at least two thoughts in mind when he gave this simile. First, it usually takes a great deal of effort and many years to amass a large fortune. Secondly, a treasure must be guarded or protected. It can be taken in an instant.

Likewise a reputation for integrity is an extremely valuable commodity. It also takes a great deal of effort and many years of commitment to obtain it. Like a treasure it has a high price tag. The whole idea of integrity implies that there are certain principles, ethics and morals that have been identified and adopted by the concerned individual. These principles then form a grid through which decisions are screened. If the decisions result in actions that conform to adopted principles, integrity has been achieved. Building a reputation of integrity demands *repeated* and *sustained* decisions to stay the course. It involves daily, moment by moment decisions to behave in accordance with ones stated beliefs.

The Road Less Traveled

Living a life of integrity is "going against the grain." It involves commitment and effort. "Doing what comes naturally" is the easier road to travel. The line of least resistance is giving in to instant gratification rather than developing deferred gratification patterns. Going the line of least resistance involves less thought, analysis or determination. Following ones impulses or going the "easy route" usually means compromising principle. Compromise can mean the surrender of ones values -- the fracturing of one's absolutes. Integrity demands suppressing the tendency to choose the easier and more convenient path. It involves a conscious decision to develop a series of core beliefs and a strong commitment to live by them. It is accompanied by perseverance -- a strong resistance to depart from the course. Since it brings great trust, people will risk their fortunes, their reputations and even their lives to follow someone with great integrity. Therefore a person of integrity is influential. A person with integrity inspires.

---

[12] *The New American Standard Bible*, (Foundation Press, La Habra, CA. 1960) Proverbs 22:1

A reputation for integrity must also be carefully guarded. Like a treasure it takes a lifetime to earn and can, tragically, be lost in a moment of time. When one loses trust due to a failure of integrity, he or she must expend great effort to earn back the respect that they have lost.

In my opinion, integrity is the "queen" of virtues. It is indeed the foundation upon which other character traits rest. The wise man, Solomon (Circa 935 BC) stated in one of his proverbs: *"The integrity of the upright will guide them."* [13] In this ancient saying, the wise man connected integrity to leadership.

---

[13] The New American Standard Bible: Proverbs 11:3; Foundation Press, La Habra, CA. 1960

Summary

Integrity is where we must begin in discussing the foundations of character for those interested in leadership. Integrity makes one complete, undivided, unimpaired. Integrity makes someone believable -- trustable. Trust is the link between integrity and leadership. From a utilitarian perspective, one interested in leadership should pursue integrity, even if he or she does not value the moral implications. Integrity earns trust. Trust is necessary to sustained leadership. It is just that simple.

Assessment

Check those items that apply:
- ❏ I do not make technically accurate statements with an intent to deceive.
- ❏ My followers have indicated that I am predictable on matters of principle.
- ❏ My actions match what I ask my followers to do.

Plan for Success:

- Which of the desirable behaviors identified in Chapter 2 (See figure 1, Page 30), are rooted in integrity?
- Identify some of your behaviors that need attention to improve to sharpen your integrity.
- Describe <u>specific actions</u> that you will take within the next 30 days to improve your commitment to integrity.

Chapter 6
<u>Courage</u>

True leaders have courage. Courage has been defined as the characteristic that allows someone to overcome a fear in order to do what one chooses to do. It implies firmness of mind and willpower in the face of danger or extreme difficulty. Integrity without courage can result in good intentions and beliefs without the consistency of action.

In a very real sense, courage cannot exist outside the presence of fear. An act or decision that involves no fear may be commendable, admirable, and even right or just; but it cannot involve courage. The very essence of the concept implies the ability to overcome an anxiety or dread that inhibits a person's behavior.

Not Without Fear

My partner and I received a "Code 2" call (urgent, but without red light and siren) about a residential burglary in progress. I was a young "rookie" with very little experience. When we arrived there were quite a few neighbors surrounding a house. They had one of the suspected burglars in custody and told us that the second criminal was still in the house. They cautioned us that the burglar in the house *could* be armed. They were unsure due to the darkness.

We requested "back up." Soon there were several units surrounding the house and a Sergeant directing the operation. My partner and I were directed to search the house while the other units maintained a parameter. The occupants of the house were on an extended vacation and had turned off the power. The house was very dark. I was scared!

With gun and flashlight in hand we carefully searched the house. I nearly shot at a huge mirror in one of the rooms when I saw myself. I could feel the hair on the back of my neck raise up. I was relieved when our search did not locate the suspect. We reported back to the Sergeant.

After consulting the neighbors, he ordered us back into the house. The neighbors were certain they had the place surrounded before he could leave. The Sergeant told us to not come out without him. We began searching again.

After looking in almost all of the probable hiding places, we still had not located our man. We started a hasty second sweep. I was in the master bedroom, *alone*. I noticed that one of the open doors was against the wall, but not completely so. It was the only place I had not examined. Could he be in such an obviously simple hiding place? I approached the door, flipped it open with my flashlight . . . and there he was!

I was startled. My leg muscles jerked involuntarily. I rose off the ground slightly. At the same time, my diaphragm caused a rapid exhale of air that made a strange noise. The funny thing was that he did exactly the same thing. After gaining control, I pointed my gun at him and ordered him to a "search" position. He was unarmed. I began to handcuff him, and we both began to laugh. The tension was relieved. We were laughing at one another and ourselves.

My partner heard the noise and came running into the room. He could not understand the laughter and wanted to know what was going on. The suspect said: "Man, did I scare your partner." He was absolutely right. But, I made my partner promise not to tell.

Later at the station, the Sergeant commended us for our capture. He said it took a lot of courage to do what we did. I disagreed, admitting to him that I was scared stiff. His response was: "That's what courage is all about - - doing what you have to do in spite of your fear. Without fear, there is no courage; maybe foolishness or being "unconscious", but not courage." I never forgot that.

True Valor

As a chief officer, for many years I sat on the Awards and Decorations Board of the Los Angeles Police Department. The duties of that board were to

Leadership: The Power of Character

review what appeared to be acts of heroism and courage by police officers and determine what, if any, formal recognition should be given. There were several levels of medals awarded for acts above and beyond the call of duty. The highest award is the "Medal of Valor." Out of hundreds of commendable actions reviewed each year by this board only a handful of these "Medals of Valor" were awarded each year.

The "Medal of Valor" was given to honor extreme actions of courage. One of the critical questions the members of the board were required to ask in evaluating this level of heroism was this: "Did the officer realize the danger he or she was facing when they made their decision that resulted in the action?" In other words, the placing of ones self "in harms way" - a place of dangerous exposure - is not enough. The concerned officer must be aware of the danger at the time of the decision. This issue is significant in understanding courage.

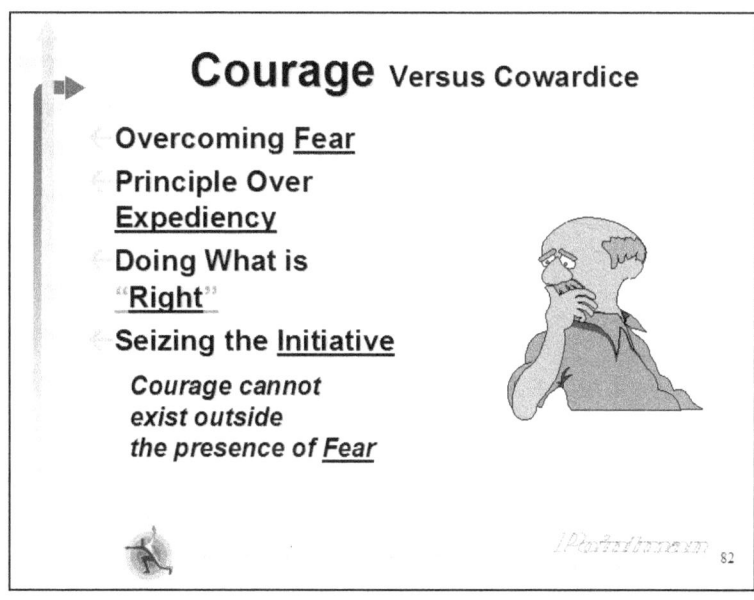

Figure 4

Courageous people are not people without fear. They are people who choose to take a course of action in spite of their fear associated with it. They are people that somehow have an inner strength that enables them to overcome their fear.

Common Fears in Leadership

Leadership exposes one to many fears. The two most common fears associated with leadership are: (1) Failure of being wrong; (2) Rejection.

When one has the power to make decisions affecting those being led there is always the possibility that he/she will be wrong. When you make decisions that can endanger financial resources, the image of the organization or the quality of life for your followers, there is always some risk involved. Any decision has the potential of being considered a "bad decision" with the passing of time and the opportunity for in depth scrutiny. For this reason many individuals resist making a decisions. They do not want to be "*wrong.*"

Often a leader must make a decision in moments, that others will have the luxury of days to consider, review and critique. This is intimidating to many that are in leadership, or aspire to it. Being "second guessed" or subjected to "Monday morning quarterbacking," can be a threatening experience. The possibility of being labeled as having poor judgment can create great fear.

Another fear common to all of us and particular to leaders is the fear of rejection. Leadership can be threatening to acceptance, friendships and approval. Decisions made by leaders are rarely popular with everyone. Decisions that are made with the effectiveness of the total organization as the primary consideration can have a perceived negative impact on an individual(s). It is virtually impossible for a leader to please all of the people all of the time. For these reasons people in leadership roles face the fear of rejection, often on a daily basis. It takes courage to overcome the strong need for acceptance and to do what is right.

Another way of dealing with the fears common to leadership is to take the road of *expediency.* The concept of expediency is characterized as a focus on a quick or easy solution without due regard for moral or ethical considerations.

Expediency can offer short term "success", immediate gratification, and reduced tension. It may be expedient to avoid a confrontation, accept an inferior work product or "bend" a rule or law. Expediency is often the easiest thing to do but it may not be the "*right*" thing to do. Doing the "*right*" thing usually involves courage. Doing the "*right*" thing may mean more diligent work, demanding a high standard be met or "going the extra mile." Courageous leaders are willing to make the tough demands, insist on compliance with the law or regulations. Courage is the strength to take the "high road."

Courage to Seize the Initiative

One of the hallmarks of great leaders is the desire to "seize the initiative." A leader is not the observer who watches things happen. The leader *makes* things happen. Seizing the initiative involves recognizing problems, seeing a window of opportunity, perceiving a vacuum of leadership and then taking action without having to be told to do so. It is widely recognized that there are many potential great leaders who never have their "day in the sun" due to a lack of opportunity. I have talked to many people who complain about not having a chance to demonstrate their leadership ability. I agree that leadership must have the "soil" of opportunity in order to "germinate." Opportunities allow latent or underutilized skills to become recognized.

Winston Churchill may not have become a well known leader had it not been for World War II. He is a well known figure of that era because he "seized the initiative", inspiring and leading the people of Britain in a desperate battle to defend their homeland.

The Chinese have an interesting view of the concept of "crisis." In their written language they have two characters they join together to represent the idea of "crisis." One of the characters represents *danger* or *hazard*. The other represents *opportunity*. From their perspective a "crisis" is a *dangerous opportunity*. From that standpoint, everyone will have great opportunities to lead. No one will deny being exposed to many crises in their lifetime. From the Chinese viewpoint, that means many opportunities – dangerous and hazardous opportunities will be there. They may be disguised as a crisis, but will in actuality be *opportunities*. The next time you are confronted with a crisis – look for the opportunity.

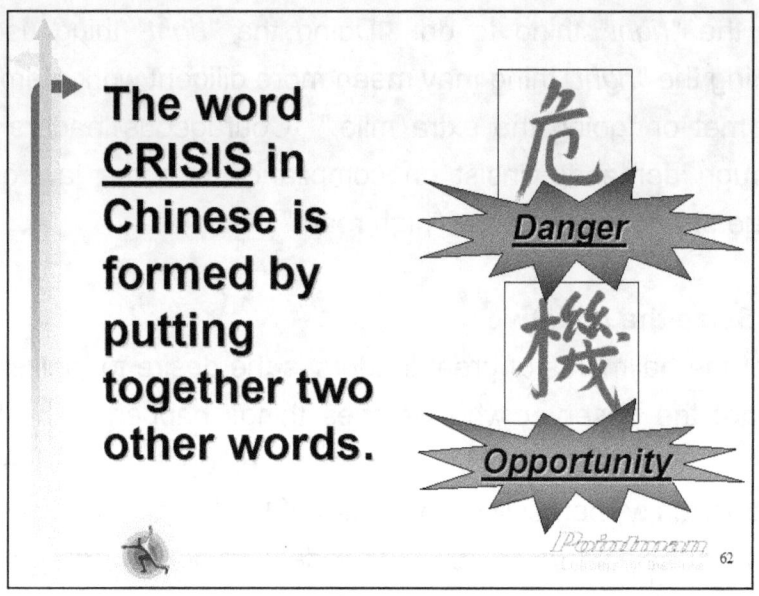

Figure 5

An Important Rendezvous

I believe everyone will intersect with a great opportunity during his or her lifetime. I believe most of us will encounter several of them. The issue is not whether or not we will have a rendezvous with a "window of opportunity", it is whether or not we will (1) recognize it as such, and then (2) seize the initiative and jump through the "window. " This requires courage.

Finally, leadership often results in what some have called, "The Loneliness of Command." Leadership can lead to a type of isolation. For example, it may not be appropriate for the leader to discuss personnel problems with anyone in the group being led. This can violate privacy considerations, create factions or give the appearance of a lack of objectivity. For this, and other reasons, many of the problems and responsibilities associated with leadership must be born alone. Developing a close social relationship or friendship with any of those being led can appear as favoritism and result in poor group morale. Accepting responsibility and having to deal with it, often in isolation, requires courage.

Summary

Courage is the character trait that allows people to overcome their fears and take the oft times risky road of leadership. It takes courage to be decisive - to run the risk of being second guessed, of failure. It takes courage to do what is "right", what is best for all concerned and face the rejection that may occur. It takes courage to seize the initiative. It takes courage to live the "Loneliness of Command." It takes courage to be a leader.

> *"Right is right, even if everyone is against it. Wrong is wrong, even if everyone is for it."* [14]

Plan for Success:
- Which of the desirable behavior identified in Chapter 2 (See Page 30), are rooted in courage?
- Identify some of your behaviors that need attention to ensure courage.
- Describe <u>specific actions</u> that you will take within the next 30 days to improve your commitment to courage.

---

[14] William Penn, American Patriot – Circa 1760

Leadership: The Power of Character

Chapter 7
Discipline

The ethic of discipline is another element in the mixture that forms the underlying foundation of a person's behavioral patterns. True leadership is always associated with discipline. Leadership is related to control. When an individual attempts to lead, he/she is asking those being led to grant control of their lives (at least on a limited basis) to them. Most people relinquish control of their lives to others rather hesitantly, to say the least. When they do, it is to someone who has demonstrated a measure of success in self-control. In the context of this discussion self-control or discipline by the leader is relevant.

The notion of discipline involves training and at times imposing sanctions to ensure compliance. The training is intended to result in a desired pattern of behavior that achieves effectiveness or excellence. Discipline is defined as:

> (1) Training that is expected to produce <u>character</u> or pattern of behavior, especially that which is expected to produce <u>moral or mental</u> improvement; (2) Controlled behavior resulting from such training.

Controlled behavior is an essential factor in true leadership.

Leadership: The Power of Character

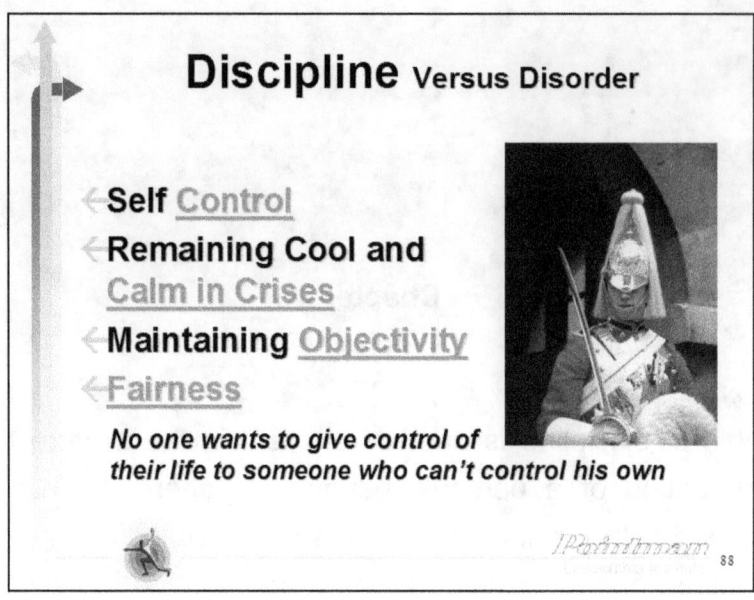

Figure 6

High Stakes and Leadership

In the police service, high-risk assignments demand strong leadership. One of the high-risk assignments is in a SWAT team (Special Weapons and Tactics). These units deal with situations where human lives are in the balance. SWAT members must work as a team and they must follow their leadership explicitly. There is usually no time for questions in a SWAT operation. Any hesitation, failure to act, or maverick action on the part of any SWAT team member can result in death and disaster. SWAT teams must have strong leadership.

One night, I received a late phone call at home. The Watch Commander at our Detective Headquarters Division notified me that two officers had been shot. I quickly dressed and started off to the scene. As I drove, I was told by police radio that the wounded officers had been taken to a hospital that was on my way to the scene. I decided to drop by and check on their condition. The deployment and tactics at the scene were being covered well by supervisors.

When I arrived, I learned how the officers were wounded. They had received a "man with a gun" call. At the scene they were told that a young man went "out of his head", got a rifle, and was running through the neighborhood naked, shooting at everything that moved. They learned that the young man had returned to his residence just prior to their arrival. They contacted his mother. She told them he was "sick" and had not been taking his medicine. She begged them not to hurt him.

They located him in his bedroom and began talking with him through the closed door. The officers tried to convince him they wished him no harm and wanted to help him.

In the haste of the moment, the mother forgot to warn the officers that there was another door to the bedroom. While the officers attempted to negotiate his surrender, he exited the room through the other door, crept up behind them and shot both of them. Both officers were seriously wounded. One had a dangerous wound to his neck, close to the spinal cord. At that time it appeared he would be a quadriplegic.

I left the hospital and headed toward the scene of the search for the suspect. I learned on the police radio that responding units had located him within the grounds of a nearby high school. They were establishing a parameter around the school. I ordered SWAT to be called out.

SWAT arrived at the FCP (Field Command Post) just moments after my arrival. Lt. Jeff Rogers, the SWAT commander, asked for his mission. I told him I wanted the assailant arrested. I explained that the suspect was probably mentally deranged and that if possible, he should be taken alive. I also made it clear that the safety of the officers should not be compromised. This was a highly charged emotional situation. Brother officers were seriously wounded. The Lieutenant accepted the mission. I watched him meet with his men. All were garbed in the black SWAT uniforms. They moved out "double time" as they deployed to the mission.

Just minutes later I heard gunfire. Then my hand held radio crackled: "*Mission accomplished. Suspect in custody. We are secure.*" I soon learned that the suspect had attempted to shoot them. They had every right to shoot-to-kill in their own self-defense but they had deliberately wounded him rather than fire lethal shots. They were under control. In spite of their strong emotional feelings about fellow officers being shot, they still followed orders.

Lieutenant Jeff Rogers was one of the most disciplined leaders on the LAPD at that time. I saw him often at the Police Academy gym when I dropped in to work out. He could outdo most of his younger team members on the pull-up bar and the bench press. His disciplined life-style was almost legendary. That was one of the primary reasons why he was selected for the demanding job of SWAT team leader. He possessed remarkable self-control. As a result he could lead his followers in the most difficult of police tactical situations, even the emotionally charged case I described.

Reducing the Risk of Following

When one decides to follow a leader, in a sense they are choosing to give control of at least a portion of their life to the leader. The follower *wills* to do what the leader is asking. Of course the goal or objective that the leader is promoting defines the extent or amount of control that the follower grants. In extreme cases, as in the police or military, those being led can actually risk death with a commitment to follow. In most leadership situations the ultimate sacrifice is not required; but there is always some measure of risk. When one grants even a small portion of control of their life to another there will be some uncertainty of outcome -- some hazard, even if ever so slight. This issue of granting control is what makes discipline necessary to leadership.

By definition, people who are disciplined have the ability to maintain self-control. They have the strength to remain calm amidst crisis. A disciplined person can resist emotional pressures and remain objective. People want leaders who have developed this inner strength. Demonstrating self-control tends to show those being led that the leader can be trusted with the control of the lives of those being led.

> **No thinking person wants to give control of his or her life (even a small portion of it) to a person who cannot control his/her own life**

Some who aspire to leadership believe they must demonstrate power by outbursts of emotion such as anger or inflexible, relentless direction. They often use crude or profane expletives to attempt to obtain compliance. Such behavior actually appears as an apparent loss of emotional control and will usually undermine a leader's influence. It may have the immediate intended result but over the long haul it will show a weakness. It will signal the dominance of emotion over reason, logic and objectivity. Of course there are situations where firm direction without discussion is appropriate; but self-control does not have to be sacrificed even on these occasions.

> "The one who guards his mouth preserves his life;
> The one who opens wide his lips comes to ruin." . . .
> Solomon 750 BC [15]

Planting and Nurturing Discipline

Once again discipline is not a character trait that just happens. I agree with early American political philosophers (Madison, Hamilton and Jay) who in *The Federalist Papers* described man in his *natural state* as selfish and brutish (*undisciplined*). Discipline is a virtue that develops through a process. The process can begin with certain levels of discipline being forced upon an individual early in life. Those fortunate to have been given a balanced mix of deliberate freedom and loving discipline soon begin to appreciate the value of discipline and choose to pursue it. Others less fortunate who either receive excessive or no

---

[15] *The New American Standard Bible*: (Foundation Press, La Habra, CA. 1960) Proverbs 13:3

discipline often resist or rebel against it. I do not believe discipline is a naturally acquired trait. It must be planted, germinated and nurtured.

The Path of Learning from Others

People who have not had the benefit of experiencing imposed discipline can observe it's valuable rewards in the lives of others. We admire those who have achieved excellence. This is especially obvious in our adulation of athletes. The results of their self-discipline and committed preparation are obvious to us. This is another way some individuals develop a desire to acquire it. They take note of its by-products and want them. They learn from the experience of others. A prerequisite for following this path is humility. One must be able to learn from listening to, or observing others and benefiting from their experience.

The Path of Logic

Finally, it is possible to desire discipline through the process of logic. Analytical people often follow this path. This process of internal motivation begins with a goal. If this type of person is strongly motivated toward a certain goal it often becomes very apparent that discipline will be required to perform the necessary tasks, acquire the knowledge or develop the skills to reach the goal. To many analytical people discipline becomes a mandatory step in their logical plan to achieve a goal. For example, athletes who strongly desire "Olympic Gold" or professional status, at some point must commit themselves to the disciplined life of training and preparation.

Regardless of the path taken, the process of developing discipline must be either imposed, or earnestly desired. If the latter is the case, the desire will be connected with some other desired outcome. Discipline is not pursued for it's own sake. Discipline is an unnatural character trait that is tolerated because it is a precursor to other desirable outcomes. Curiously, the practice of discipline often leads to embracing it. This is not because it is natural, but due to its rewards. For example, studies have shown that people who exercise the discipline of preparing written goals (even a daily "to do list") accomplish much more than those who do not.

Bite Off a Small Piece

I have observed that those who are the most successful in practicing the process of developing discipline follow a basic principle. This is the principle of planning gradual and progressively more difficult challenges. In other words they begin modestly and celebrate realistic and achievable goals. Then they move on to moderate and eventually more difficult objectives. Most of us err in taking a step larger or more difficult than we should and then give up when we experience defeat.

When I began my running program many years ago, my initial goal was to jog 50 strides and then walk 50 paces until I completed a half-mile course. I could do that. Gradually, I increased the challenge until I was jogging three miles per day. That gradual process took several months. I have talked to people who have begun an exercise program with an overly ambitious schedule. In these situations, failure is almost certain. Injuries or profound discomfort can result. When this occurs the person usually wants to give up entirely.

Summary

Leadership involves controlling the lives of others. Self-control or discipline is one of the ethics or character traits that gives the leader the right to ask for others to grant that power to them. Discipline is admired and followed. Developing discipline in any area of one's life is difficult. It is going "upstream." It is against human nature and therefore it always involves some stress. I strongly believe that the stress in this case is beneficial and worth the investment. The difficult and often stressful process of developing discipline in one's character is worth the effort, because the rewards are so great.

Plan for Success:

- Which of the desirable behaviors identified in Chapter 2 (See page 30), are rooted in discipline?
- Identify some of your behaviors that need attention to ensure discipline.
- Describe <u>specific actions</u> that you will take within the next 30 days to improve your commitment to discipline.
- Identify some "small steps" you can begin within 30 days.

Chapter 8
Loyalty – In Order to Lead, I Must also Follow

I was on my way to Mongolia with instructors from Germany and England. At the start of a two-day layover in Beijing, we were met at the airport, driven to a five-star hotel, and escorted to a private room where I was introduced to a three-star general who called me "General Vernon." I explained that there were no generals in the LAPD; my title was Assistant Chief of Police.

"How many men were under your command?" an interpreter asked.

"Eight thousand, ten thousand including civilians," I answered.

"Then you are a general."

That evening, we had a long conversation over a twelve-course dinner. I was aware that the government was considering whether or not to invite me to do a seminar for their police chiefs. This evening was an important step in the process. Between courses, the Chinese general cordially asked me many questions about my experience in the LAPD. The questions indicated that a lot of research had been done on my background. For example, "General Vernon, in 1972, when you were Captain of Venice precinct, you had a problem with a small riot. What principles and strategies did you use to quell the riot?"

I felt good about our conversation as the twelfth course was served--hot fudge sundaes in my honor, they explained. After the desert dishes were removed, the general spoke again. "The news reports in your country are saying that China has been stealing intellectual property." I knew he was referring to music CDs, movie DVDs, and computer chips that were being pirated and distributed without royalty. "General Vernon, would you give me your opinion, please?"

I sensed that this was a major test, and implied was a double standard--that piracy of intellectual property was occurring in the United States, too.

"General, before I answer your question, I need to give you an ancient proverb. The proverb is: 'Better are wounds from a friend than kisses from an enemy.'"

The general nodded and smiled.

"The reason I give the general this proverb is because I'm about to wound him. We understand what is going on in China. I believe that here in China your police power is much more absolute than ours in America. Therefore, if you wanted to stop this problem, you could." The general stiffened and a hiss of air escaped from his lips. "Therefore, it is my opinion, and that of most Americans who know about this issue, that you are doing what we call 'winking the eye.' You are ignoring this and allowing it to happen."

The general's face blanched and he began to speak rapidly. The interpreter worked hard to "keep up" as the general proceeded to tell me how the United States was exploiting third world countries and exporting imperialism through capitalism. After several minutes of this tirade, I held up the palm of my hand to his face and said, "Stop!" I knew this would be considered an insult, but I had to speak. "General, I am here as your guest. But you are saying negative things about my country, and I'm offended. I love my country. I pray I'd have the courage to die for my country if it became necessary. So please do not insult my country."

The general stood and spoke sharply to his interpreter, then led the rest of his entourage out of the room. My two associates, the interpreter and myself were all that remained. We stared at each other for a moment, embarrassed. Then I asked the government interpreter, "What just happened--when the general spoke to you?"

The translator smiled and said, "The general has told me to tell you that your seminar is approved!"

One of my associates from Germany couldn't resist saying, "Herr General, you have passed the test!"

I was still trying to comprehend what had happened. "What do you mean?"

Leadership: The Power of Character

"All of the questions covered each of the principles of character that we teach in the seminar. The last test was on *loyalty*. The general was testing you to see if you believed it, or if it was just something nice to teach."

The Quality of Faithfulness

I hadn't realized just how valued loyalty was in other cultures until that experience, or how unusual it is. By loyalty, I mean being faithful to one's country or superior in a "chain of command." This trait is important because in order to lead, one must have followers. The most powerful way to obtain a following is to model that behavior -- in other words to be a good follower yourself.

Loyalty results in many of the behaviors people desire to see in their leader. A loyal leader is *responsive* and accepts the responsibility of being a *champion of* his or her followers. A leader with this character trait *gives recognition* to whom it is due rather than accepting the glory. He/she also works hard at removing the barriers confronting their followers. Loyalty is essential to powerful leadership.

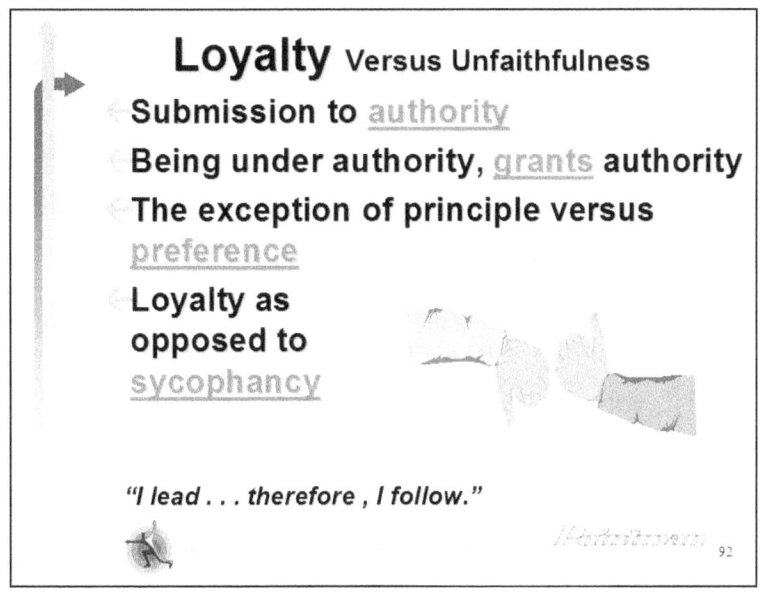

Figure 7

Submission to authority is the core issue in loyalty. As one submits to his/her authority, in a real sense they are letting authority flow through them. Said another way, if leaders desire authority, they must submit to it. When someone complains to me that he is experiencing a problem with subordinates failing to recognize his/her authority, my inquiry focuses on his/her relationship to the authority over him/her. Often the problem is due to his/her own lack of respect or submission to authority.

When I first read the statement at the bottom of Figure 7 ("I lead . . . therefore I follow") many years ago, I did not understand the principle behind the statement. In fact, it seemed like a contradiction. However, I have grown to understand the powerful principle in this simple statement. I learned this principle through a set of circumstances that nearly led to disaster.

The "Good Friday" Shooting.

Late afternoon on "Good Friday," (a religious day during the Easter season) my adjutant interrupted a meeting to notify me of a major gang incident with multiple murders. Immediately I was driven to the scene. Yellow tape was already up establishing the perimeter of the crime scene. Scores of neighbors were gathered outside the police line. Cameramen and reporters from the media were being led by a press relations officer through the taped off area to an appropriate location near the focus of attention. Several ambulances, lights flashing, were still being loaded with the wounded.

Members of my staff and one of the detectives in charge of the investigation led me to the center of the crime scene. Shell casings were circled with chalk or covered with paper cones to protect them from pollution or destruction. Several bodies were covered with sheets. It was a scene of carnage that paled most of my thirty-eight years of police experience. Two gang members using assault rifles had cut down at least ten people. Among the victims was a young, innocent child--a bystander caught up in the senseless slaughter.

On Monday morning I was summoned to Chief Gates office. He was visibly upset about the tragedy of Friday. With genuine passion, he discussed the increasing violence and gave me three missions to address the problem. First, he wanted me to form a thousand-officer special enforcement unit. We would call this special deployment "The Hammer Task Force." We would deploy this massive unit over and above the officers normally deployed in the area (about 350 officers) on selected days and nights. They would work in the area most plagued by gang warfare. Our mission would be to legally and professionally target the gang members. Through "probable cause", pro-active police work, we would arrest as many gang members as possible and hopefully seize their weapons before they could be used again. I accepted this bold mission with enthusiasm.

Secondly, I was directed to dramatically increase the numbers of personnel devoted to "Operation Jeopardy." This strategy was a means of identifying young people associating with known gang members before they became hardened members themselves. It involved specially trained juvenile officers making discreet notification to the parents of these "at risk" juveniles. Services and support were offered. The program was very popular and appreciated in the community. I was in complete agreement with the Chief in his wise decision to implement a balanced approach to the gang problem. "Operation Jeopardy" would balance out the tough, no nonsense, yet very needed approach of "The Hammer."

Finally, Chief Gates asked me to implement a program with another county agency that I personally did not think valuable or effective. We had talked about this program for several weeks. He had listened to my objections carefully and patiently. On this day he gave firm direction to me to implement it immediately. I again voiced my objections, and then reluctantly accepted his order.

I called for a 4:00PM meeting of the commanding officers of the city's five police bureaus. Fortunately, it was impossible for two of the chief officers to attend. We eventually scheduled the meeting for the following morning at the police academy restaurant. The delay in the meeting was fortunate because I had initially intended to compromise the direction given to me by the Chief of Police. I was ready to vigorously pursue the first two missions. But I disagreed with the third mission and I was actually contemplating watering down the efforts needed to accomplish it. I considered telling my five subordinate officers (my followers) not to take the third mission seriously--to perhaps give it minimal attention; report some efforts in the activity reports to the Chief, but not to put their hearts into it.

Fortunately, that night I thought better of my flawed decision. I recalled the quote that at one time had puzzled to me. *"I lead . . . therefore I follow,"* was directly applicable to this situation. The next morning, during the breakfast meeting with my followers, I fully supported all three of the Chief's directives. If I had withheld my full support for all three of the Chief's orders, I would have modeled a disloyal follower and I would have taught my followers to be disloyal to me. Leading by example is the most powerful way we lead.

Submitting to "Turkeys"

Chief Ed Davis was the Chief of Police in Los Angeles through much of the 1970's. He was a very capable administrator who had a good grasp of leadership. He understood the principles of authority and did his best to operate within them. During Davis' tenure the City used a commission system to oversee the many city departments. Then Mayor, Tom Bradley, appointed five citizens to the Police Commission who were oriented toward the liberal side of the political spectrum. Chief Davis was known for his often flamboyant statements that were interpreted by most as leaning toward the conservative position. This seemed to be an obvious set-up for a confrontational relationship that would be rife with discord and strife.

Chief Davis understood power. In practically all public statements, he gave not only respect for the institution of the Commission but its members as well. He rarely openly disagreed with them except within the bounds of propriety. For example, he always invited a member of the Commission to participate in graduation ceremonies of the current recruit class at the police academy. I viewed this action as significant. I knew how jealously he guarded any input to those he regarded as his "off-spring." In those circumstances he always introduced Commission members with great respect and deference. Many of us were aware that the Chief did not share many of the positions the Commission took on matters of policy. Yet he neither denigrated them or their position. He submitted to their authority.

Ed Davis was a powerful chief who accomplished many effective changes in the Department. He was successful in accomplishing a major structural as well as philosophical change in the LAPD now known as Community Based Policing. Being able to execute such a major change in a large bureaucracy is indicative of powerful leadership skills. I believe his understanding the nature of authority and his submission to it was at the heart of his effectiveness in this regard.

When Chief Davis retired there was a huge retirement party at the Century Plaza Hotel. Several thousand people attended. It was a gala affair. Several days later a private dinner was held at the Chatsworth Country Club. All staff officers (those above the rank of Captain) were invited. There were about forty of us in attendance. At the close of the evening, the Chief delivered his personal farewell speech. At the conclusion of this intimate "good bye," he shouted: "I'm finally out from *under* those 'turkeys!'" He at last candidly expressed his frustration of having to work under a chain of command that was often in opposition to his own ideology. We found out later that behind closed doors, in the executive sessions, Chief Davis often disagreed with his "bosses." But he chose to make his arguments confidential and not a source of divisiveness within the Department.

Several weeks later a young captain came into my office. He noticed that I had a picture of retired Chief Davis on my wall. It was a picture of the Chief in his dress uniform with all of the pomp and circumstance, including the four stars on his shoulders and the "scrambled eggs" on his cap bill. The Chief had written some kind words to me on the photograph and I was proud to display it. The Captain remarked: "Who's that funny looking guy with that funny looking uniform?"

Of course he knew who it was. Davis had left office only two weeks prior. The Captain was making a statement. He was saying *Ed Davis does not have any power over me anymore. Neither he nor his uniform intimidates me.*

Yes, Ed Davis had . . . "gotten out from under" the Commission. But in so doing, he had also removed himself from the flow of power. Stepping out from under authority removes you from the flow of authority. Conversely, submitting to proper authority places you in the position of empowerment.

When Saying "No" to the Boss is Right

There is one important exception to submitting to authority and it involves the issue of principle. When one is asked to deviate from an important moral principle or violate the law, the answer must be "No." However, these situations are usually rare and one must use extreme discretion in negotiating these difficult waters. Even a well-meaning error here can have severe repercussions.

In refusing to submit to authority, one must first determine that the request actually violates a *principle* and not just a *preference*. The key focus here should be classifying the issue correctly. I tend to hastily classify something I object to as a violation of principle. Most of the time, as I reflect over the issues, I must honestly admit the matter *is* one of preference. The distinction is of utmost importance, for refusing to submit to authority when it is not an issue of principle will result in the loss of power.

Principles that justify disobeying or subverting authority must be based on some tangible precept. A violation of the law or the breaking of widely accepted social standards, such as the time tested "Ten Commandments", would qualify. In my opinion the nebulous plea of "conscience" cannot justify insubordination unless it is based upon the above.

Let's suppose that I was asked by the Chief of Police to represent the Police Department before the City Council on the negotiation of our annual budget. Suppose the Chief asked me to lie about how we intended to spend the funds on a particular program and further to deceive the Council if they began probing the issue. (I want to make it clear that I never had to confront this scenario). In this situation I would decline and make it clear the way I interpreted the request or direction. In other words I would suggest saying: "Boss, are you asking me to lie . . . to purposely deceive the City Council?" The important function of this tactic is to graphically classify the request for what it is -- an unlawful order. At this point the superior officer may well "back track" and the confrontation will be over. But if it is not resolved in this way, a person of integrity may absolutely refuse to follow the direction and bear the responsibility for that refusal.

Of course, when a subordinate refuses to follow the unlawful or immoral direction of his/her boss, there is the possibility of reprisal. Usually this will *not* occur since the superior does not want to make public what he/she has asked you to do. But even though some negative fallout does occur, your integrity is preserved and even the misguided superior has learned about an important and valuable component of your character. Although he/she may be angry and frustrated at the time, this personal experience can be the basis for increased trust in the long run. That same immoral superior may well turn to you when he/she really wants someone they can trust.

I have had people suggest that this idea of loyalty does not apply in their case since their boss is "unreasonable." The notion of being *unreasonable* involves a value judgment that in my opinion does not qualify as a *principled* excuse. An ancient writing, nearly 2000 year old, states: *" Submit (to an employer or superior), not only to those who are kind and good; but also to those who are unreasonable."*[16] *Refusing* to submit to authority based solely upon a subjective evaluation of the person in authority or the issue at point must be seen for what it is - - disloyalty and disobedience.

When "Yes" is Wrong

On the other hand, loyalty does not mean sycophantic behavior. A sycophant is defined as: "*a servile, self seeking flatterer; a parasite.*" [17] This is

---

[16] *The New American Standard Bible*: (Foundation Press, La Habra, CA. 1960) 1 Peter 2:18

[17] *Webster's 7th New Collegiate Dictionary*; (G & C. Merriam Company 1965)

the type of person who seeks to curry favor with the "boss" by always agreeing with him/her. Sycophants give the superior officer positive feedback, even when they know he/she is wrong or about to make a mistake. This is not loyalty. This is dishonest praise that is destructive rather than supportive. While presenting this material at a seminar in Kenya, the participants stated: "In Kenya we call such a person a 'boot licker'."

Sometimes the most loyal act a follower can give their leader is an honest and clear word of warning or disagreement. Of course this must be done with respect. I learned early in my career in the "executive suite" that often this faithful act must be done confidentially. The best setting for a candid criticism is not during a staff meeting. It is difficult for most leaders to accept disapproval or apparent rejection in front of a room full of subordinates. Discretion in this duty may demand patience.

There is an ancient proverb that sums up the essence of this perspective on loyalty. "*Better is open rebuke than love that is concealed. Faithful are the wounds of a friend, but deceitful are the kisses of an enemy*." [18] This wise saying graphically explains that on occasion a real friend, a loyal person, will tell the truth even when it causes discomfort. A loyal person will give straightforward opinions and reactions to his leader for the welfare of that leader, as well as the overall good of the organization. However, once this valuable information has been provided, the final decision of the leader must be followed.

Another word of caution is necessary at this point. Sometimes we have the wrong motive for disagreeing with the leader. Some of us provide criticism in order to make ourselves look good or justify our natural instinct of rebellion. I must admit, I have fooled myself in justifying resistance to authority under the guise of providing loyal dissent. In reality on some of these occasions I have enjoyed being "the devil's advocate." I think we have all known people who seem to delight in explaining why direction from above will not work. Loyalty is

---

[18] *The New American Standard Bible*: (Foundation Press, La Habra, CA. 1960) Proverbs 13:3

genuine when the real reason for dissent or criticism is selfless and the motive is pure. It is legitimate when it is intended to be helpful and constructive.

Loyalty does not desire to destroy or hinder. It strives to protect, to support and to improve. Resistance to authority that does not have these goals in mind cannot be classified as loyalty. It must be recognized for what it is - - destructive rebellion. It is my opinion that a loyalty deficit in a supposed leader is the most likely reason for a lack of followers. In order for the leader to have loyal followers – he/she must be loyal.

Leadership: The Power of Character

Summary

The ethic of loyalty means the leader submits to the authority above him/her. Authority is essential to effective leadership. Therefore, the ethic of loyalty must be pursued and valued by all those seeking to lead. This important virtue places one *under* the flow of power. As a result, the power flows through them. The leader must demonstrate to his/her followers the discipline of following. This act of loyalty teaches others how to follow. This principle demonstrates that in order to lead, one must follow.

Assessment

Check those items that apply:
- ❑ Those under me willingly submit to my authority.
- ❑ I have demonstrated loyalty to those in authority over me.
- ❑ When I disagree with my superior, it is always based on principle.
- ❑ I am responsive to my team and represent them well to my superior.
- ❑ I willingly give the recognition due members of my team.
- ❑ I identify and remove work barriers for my team.
- ❑ I am a model of submission to authority to those around me.

Plan for Success:
- Which of the desirable behaviors identified in Chapter 2 (See page 30) are rooted in loyalty?
- Identify some of your behaviors that need attention to ensure loyalty.
- Describe <u>specific actions</u> that you will take within the next 30 days to improve your commitment to loyalty.

Chapter 9
Diligence

Diligence in one's work is highly desired by many, especially those hiring workers and employers. Yet it is becoming more difficult to find. During the last several decades there has been erosion of the "work ethic." Some have even berated it as "old fashioned" and describe workers who have this trait as naive and foolish.

In the early days of America, a person worked hard and with devotion to achieving excellence in his/her craft because they felt it was moral and admirable. Taking pride in one's work was held up as a desirable attitude -- a noble course to pursue. Diligence was actually a component of religious life. In my opinion, this unusual integration of religious devotion and practical hard work resulted in the unprecedented rapid rise of America as a world power.

I believe the triumph of the West over atheistic Communism was largely accomplished by the ethic of diligence in one's work. Work in Western Judeo/Christian culture was a means of demonstrating one's piety and commitment to his/her spiritual faith. Work was viewed as a "calling;" a means to bring honor to one's God. Being connected to a transcending spiritual commitment brought importance and meaning to work. Work was more than a method of "bringing home the bacon." It was one of the most important factors in bringing relevance and purpose to life.

Max Weber described what he called "the Protestant ethic" in his classic book "The Rise of Capitalism and the Protestant Ethic." According to Weber, diligence in one's work was an integral part of this ethic. In the Bible, followers of Jesus Christ were urged to work with all diligence as a clear manifestation of their true faith. They were instructed to work as though their boss was the Lord Himself. This ethic is described in the Bible as one who not only works hard when being observed by others or their immediate supervisor, but also when no

Leadership: The Power of Character

one is looking. In this sense it is described as a virtue that will ultimately reap favorable results because it is the "right" thing to do.

> *"Don't work hard only when your master (employer) is watching and then shirk when he isn't looking; work hard and with gladness all the time, as though working for Christ, doing the will of God."* . . . .
> . . .*Paul of Antioch Circa 60 AD* [19]

Figure 8

The Pursuit of Excellence

Diligence also involves the pursuit of excellence. This is indeed a noble effort. And the phrase "pursuit of excellence" is a good one. In a sense one never arrives. As one level of excellence is achieved, it enables one to reach for an even higher level of excellence. Our word *excellence comes* from the Latin

---

[19] The Living Bible; (Tyndale House Publishers) Ephesians 6:6,7

root *cellere,* meaning to rise. It implies a process of gaining new heights -- of a continual reaching for higher levels of accomplishment or unending improvement. Excellence becomes a life style.

Gary Inrig makes an important observation about excellence. He sees a distinguishing factor about it that takes it above accomplishment.

> "Excellence is not a great accomplishment or a marvelous performance. True excellence is a way of life. It touches all that we are and all that we do. Too often excellence is thought of in the narrowest of terms. An athlete pursues a championship trophy; a businessman seeks a quality product; an author strives to develop his skills as he works on his masterpiece. But this striving may not flow over into other areas of life. The result is impressive accomplishments but an inconsistent life. True excellence, which reflects the character of our God, touches all of life until it becomes a way of life." [20]

Excellence is superior to success. There are many significant differences between *success and excellence.* One can be successful without achieving excellence. For example, a world class Olympic sprint athlete can win a race without achieving excellence. Theoretically this athlete could challenge a group of spectators to compete against him in his chosen sport. If the spectators were a typical representation of average adults, the Olympic athlete would no doubt be successful in the competition without achieving excellence. That is, he could run the race and cross the finish line first without running his absolute best. To achieve excellence he would have to do his very best, rather than just perform a little better than the fastest competitor. Excellence involves reaching for the full potential.

Organizations that achieve high levels of accomplishment have excellence as one of the components of their culture. The "way of life" of excellence permeates everything they do. When excellence is adopted as an organizational

---

[20] Gary Inrig *A Call to Excellence*: (Victor Books, Wheaton Ill. 1985) p 9

value, people in the organization are ignited by it. An atmosphere of excellence is contagious, motivating and fulfilling. In fact, it can be so strong a force that individuals that do not measure up are not tolerated. We have all seen athletic teams that just do not tolerate mediocrity.

> *"Excellence in any art or profession is attained only by hard and persistent work."* — Theodore Martin

The leader has the primary responsibility of "sowing the seeds" of excellence in his/her followers. Once again the most effective way to do this is to model excellence and reward those who embrace it. Talk is cheap. Actions powerfully communicate this ethic. The leader must demonstrate commitment to excellence in his/her personal life as well as deliberately and publicly giving positive reinforcement to those who follow. He/she must retain the focus on this important concept.

Is Excellence "Dangerous?"

A departure from this way of thinking has been encouraged by several institutions in our society. Many educational systems have surrendered the goal of excellence and adopted "more realistic goals" that accommodate the lowest common denominator. Some have even berated the pursuit of excellence as divisive and humiliating to those who either will not or cannot achieve it. Team achievement rather than individual accomplishment is emphasized. Adherents of this perverted logic explain that the "dangerous" emphasis of high achievement can make non-achievers "feel bad" and give up.

The cult of the "self-image" zealots apparently believe that it is more important to feel good about one's self than to accomplish something. They place more emphasis on artificially manufactured *positive feelings* rather than legitimate fulfillment obtained through disciplined struggle and hard won victory. Gone is the adage that everything of real value has a price that must be paid. This phenomenon is connected to an overall departure from holding individuals responsible for their actions or lack thereof.

Some in the union movement have replaced the goals of high productivity and quality work with job security and increased employment. Workers in jobs controlled by unions often see priorities based on technical adherence to labor rules rather than the idea of doing their very best. Administrative law is also evolving to place more emphasis on "workers rights." High standards demanded by excellence are sacrificed in the interest of "rights." The idea of individual responsibility and commensurate rewards or sanctions has all but disappeared from many work situations.

Hard Working Cops Get Lucky

When I first entered police work, an old Irish Sergeant explained a maxim of the trade. I had remarked about how lucky a couple of officers had been in arresting a bandit on the "most wanted list." He responded: "Hard working cops get 'lucky'." I had to think about that for a few moments until I grasped his meaning. With a sly grin on his face he explained: "It's amazing that the more rocks you turn over, the more snakes you find." He went on to encourage me to work diligently and reap the resulting benefits.

My thirty-eight years of police experience validated what that old Sergeant had taught me. A sincere commitment to pursuing excellence in one's work does have many benefits. When I applied myself diligently to my work, I experienced good results. I became more effective; my supervisors gave me recognition; I felt fulfilled.

The Commanding Officer of LAPD's Wilshire Area invited me as Assistant Chief of Police, to participate in a recognition ceremony at his police station. Several officers were given commendations. One officer was recognized for a significant accomplishment. He was given a plaque for establishing a new record for the number of "hot roller" arrests in one month. The phrase "hot roller" refers to arresting a car thief while he is actually driving a stolen car. Recovering a stolen car without the car thief is referred to as "plucking a sitting duck." It is difficult to spot, successfully stop and arrest a "hot roller." The officer being recognized had made 13 "hot roller" arrests in one month. Understanding that a typical patrol officer works less than 15 days a month, considering days off, court appearances and training, this is an amazing accomplishment.

After the awards ceremony everyone joined in a brief celebration, feasting on cakes baked by grateful citizens from the community served. I approached the officer who had been awarded the plaque for setting a new "hot roller" record. I asked him what was the secret of his success. He pointed to his eyes stating: "Have you noticed I am wearing contacts?"

I responded, "Not really, does that have something to do with it?"

"Yes", he explained, "While my partner drives, I "run" practically every car we pass on the MDT " (referring to the on-board computer in our police cars). My head has been so much into the computer screen that I developed eye strain and now must wear corrective lenses." Then he added, "Chief, the more you check, the better the odds you will score."

Although this may be taking things to the extreme, he was right of course. Diligent work does pay off. But how is this virtue connected to leadership? The answer is simple. Every leader with any sense would like to have his/her followers endowed with this work ethic. The most powerful way to encourage this ethic is to model it. Leading by example with this virtue is not only effective in persuading one's followers; it makes the leader more productive in the tasks of leading. And many functions of leadership are just that -- tasks to be done. Leadership is not so much that nebulous trait of "Charisma" as it is diligent "homework" in developing the character traits that we are discussing. Hard working leaders get "lucky" in accomplishing their objectives. In so doing, they establish a "culture" of excellence. This is one of the most important responsibilities of leadership – establishing the cultural matrix for followers.

Leadership: The Power of Character

Summary

Diligence is a necessary component in the effective leader's character. It makes it possible for the leader to develop to his/her full potential. More importantly, diligence on the part of the leader becomes contagious. It germinates a **culture** that can provide an environment where hard work and excellence become a way of life.

Assessment

Check those items that apply:
- ☐ Excellence is a way of life rather than a specific goal.
- ☐ I achieve much satisfaction and fulfillment from work.
- ☐ I am committed toward doing my best even when alone and unobserved.

Plan for Success:
- Which of the desirable behaviors identified in Chapter 2 (see page 30), are rooted in diligence?
- Identify some of your behaviors that need attention to ensure diligence.
- Describe specific actions that you will take within the next 30 days to improve your commitment to diligence.

Leadership: The Power of Character

Chapter 10
Humility

Of all the ethics we will discuss, humility is perhaps the one most apt to be overlooked as supportive of strong leadership. At first blush, humility may seem to be inconsistent with strong conviction or the courageous risk-taking that is necessary for leadership. Humility has a perverted meaning to many. Webster's dictionary defines this ethic as: (1) " *not proud or haughty; not arrogant.*" However the dictionary recognizes another meaning that can attach to this word (2): " . . . *humble may also imply undue self-depreciation.*" In the context of this book, I refer to the primary definition. [21]

Being haughty or arrogant is dysfunctional to inspiring leadership. People resist willingly following someone who has a closed mind to their ideas or suggestions. On the contrary, they enjoy being able to contribute their insights to someone seeking their support.

True humility makes someone teachable. This ethic allows one to have an "open mind." A humble person honestly believes that they do not have all of the information or knowledge on a given subject. They look upon life as an experience of continued learning. They acknowledge the fact that it is impossible for anyone to "know all." This recognition can lead one to be open to new ideas, different insights and even opposing opinions.

---

[21] *Webster's 7th New Collegiate Dictionary*; (G & C. Merriam Company 1965)

The Disease of "Allness."

Professor, Dr. William Haney, a communication specialist at Northwestern University, labels one of the classic obstacles to clear communication as "allness." He defines "allness" as an attitude that hinders good communication based upon two assumptions:

(1) It is possible to know and say everything about something.
(2) What I am saying (or writing or thinking) includes all that is important about the subject. [22]

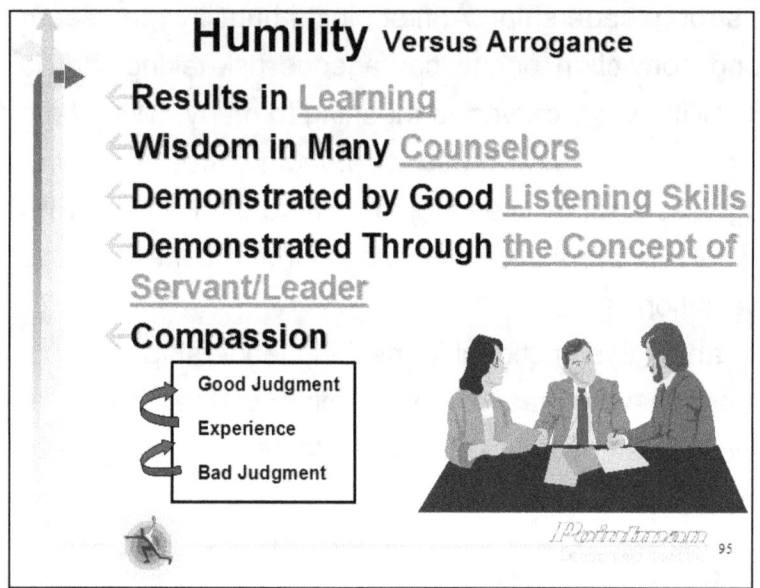

Figure 9

These are faulty assumptions. **No one** can know everything there is to know about a given topic or subject. True humility can be a significant step toward eliminating this hindrance. As a matter of fact, people low in a hierarchy often have the most detailed information about a given subject. This is because

---

[22] William Haney *Communication & Organizational Behavior* P253

they are actually doing the work and have the opportunity to develop expertise within their limited sphere of activity.

An ancient proverb states: " *Plans go wrong with too few counselors; many counselors bring success.*" [23] The basic notion here is that success in any venture depends upon an openness to consider many perspectives and opinions. Although this axiom seems obvious, human nature tends to lead toward a closed mind. I must admit my first impulse is to assume my own life experience and acquired knowledge will be sufficient. This typical and impulsive approach to leadership inevitably leads to problems and even failure.

On the other hand, a leader who maintains an open mind is able to accumulate more information. The more information one has on an issue, the more likely a good decision will be made. Accumulating and evaluating additional data can result in the opportunity to generate multiple alternatives in the decision making process. It stands to reason that comparing and selecting the best alternative from many, is superior to a limited "closed-minded" approach.

Developing expertise in a specific area of knowledge or skill takes a lifetime. In police work it takes decades to develop a homicide investigator with effective and respected skills in that type of investigation. In the trades it also takes years of experience to attain the status of master craftsman. Likewise in the professions there is no substitute for experience.

Leaders are limited

People who pursue the challenge of leadership rarely come from a career involving specialized expertise. Rather they specialize in leadership. Typically they have been involved on a "fast track" of establishing a variety of experiences at the operating level. Occasionally, they move into leadership after having some experience in a specific area of specialization. If they have developed expertise through extensive experience, it is limited to a narrow specialized field. People in leadership are usually individuals with a little experience in a variety of

---

[23] The New American Standard Bible: Proverbs 15:22; Foundation Press, La Habra, CA. 1960

disciplines. In other words a "Jack of all trades; but master of none." They may have expertise in one of the functions they supervise; but lack knowledge in all the others. In either case they are limited in their knowledge and experience.

Leaders are therefore people having limited information about the tasks performed by the people they are leading. They either know a little about what most of their followers are doing; or they know a lot about what one particular group of their followers is doing. In the first instance, they must depend upon everyone to fill in their lack of expertise in every area. In the latter, they must depend upon those outside of their own expertise to support their complete lack of experience in the other operations of the enterprise.

In order to be an effective leader, one must draw on the expertise of those he/she is leading. The failure to recognize this basic principle of leadership is the most common cause of bad decisions by those in authority.

On one of my "ride along" experiences with a street police officer we were involved in the pursuit of a dangerous robbery suspect. He had robbed a convenience store. During the robbery he had fired shots at the victim. He was escaping in a stolen car when a black and white radio car from our Venice district spotted him and began broadcasting their pursuit. Along with my partner for the day, I was enjoying a special luncheon prepared by some grateful ladies in South Central Los Angeles. There were a total of about fifteen officers at this special appreciation luncheon. Suddenly we heard the distinctive three beeps on our LAPD Rover "walkie talkie" type radio. In LAPD radio protocol, three beeps means a "hot shot" broadcast is about to follow. My partner turned up the volume and we listened intently.

"All units on all frequencies stand by – 14 A 37 is in pursuit".

Then we heard the voice of one of the officers in the unit.

"14 A 37, we are in pursuit of the 211 (armed robbery) vehicle northbound on Centinella Blvd."

They were going fast – the tone of the voice of the officer broadcasting was high pitched.

One of the officers stated: "Going about 80, huh Chief?"

I nodded my head in agreement.

We stopped eating and focused on the pursuit. Suddenly we realized they were coming our way. We were at 111th and Hoover. We heard them broadcast their position on 111th at Bering Cross and realized they were just blocks away. All fifteen ran out the door and rounded the corner of the building. The bandit was really down on his luck. He had just decided he was far enough ahead of the pursuing police unit to bail out of his stolen car and get lost in the neighborhood. All fifteen of us appeared just as he hit the sidewalk.

He jumped over a fence trying desperately to escape. We quickly formed a parameter abound the area of houses just as one of our helicopters joined the operation. The chopper told us he had crawled under a house. I requested a K9 unit to "ferret" him out rather than get an officer shot.

While we were waiting for the officer with the police dog to arrive my Rover radio crackled.

"Officer in front of the white house with the black ford pick-up in the driveway, please move one house to your east, sir".

I realized he was directing me to move. He was a "two striper" – six or seven levels below me in rank. But of course, I responded, "Yes sir". He had a better perspective than I did. From his position in the sky above, he could see the whole parameter. I would have been foolish to refuse to listen or comply because of my superior rank. The armed bandit was apprehended shortly.

This story illustrates an important truth. Often those below a leader in rank, seniority, age or education have a unique position that gives them a superior perspective on a specific issue.

When You Don't Know What You are Doing

When I was promoted to the rank of Lieutenant, my captain told me I would be assigned as a Watch Commander of the Accident Investigation Division. This division was responsible for investigating traffic accidents. I would be responsible for commanding a "watch" -- meaning an eight-hour period of time. Over 200 uniformed officers and a contingent of "plain clothes" detectives were deployed to this elite assignment. Officers in this division were hand picked from those seeking this assignment after establishing a superior record as a generalist patrol officer. They received specialized training and were assigned with a seasoned investigator during their first year of on the job training. In other words, I would be commanding people with expertise in traffic investigations. I had never worked as a traffic specialist and had avoided traffic work as a generalist. I had no expertise in this field whatsoever.

As previously explained in Chapter two, I told my captain that I would rather not be assigned to a traffic division and asked if I had any other options. His response was that if I had any ideas of further promotions, I should be "happy" to accept this assignment. He told me they had noted that I had no traffic experience. He reasoned that since traffic is a major responsibility of the police profession, anyone rising to the executive level should have some traffic experience.

Of course I accepted the assignment, but asked: "How can I lead an operation where I have no experience?"

The captain advised: "There are several excellent "old time" sergeants who have spent their whole time on the job in 'A.I.' . Sergeant Hal Bonner knows just about everything there is to know about this specialty. If I were you, I would seek out his assistance. Admit to him you are inexperienced and need his support."

Then the captain gave me simple but profoundly wise counsel.

"Vernon, one of the most powerful requests is found in the simple question: 'Will you help me?' I suggest you admit to your sergeants that you need them. Admit your deficiencies. Humbly ask for their assistance. Let them know you are depending on them."

That was good advice. That experience illustrated to me the importance of the leadership ethic of **humility**. When I followed his advise the sergeants were pleased and seemed to delight in helping the "wet behind the ears" lieutenant who needed them. When I didn't I was less effective.

It is equally important for one to be able to learn from his/her own mistakes and failures. Humility makes it possible for this to happen.

The Formula for Good Judgment

Many years ago I saw the formula depicted in figure #8 hanging on the wall behind the desk of an important executive. I was intrigued by it; but honestly did not grasp its full meaning until my friend explained it to me. It explains a powerful process if one has the humility to follow it.

The formula states that *good judgment* is a result of *experiences;* and *experience* is a result of *bad judgment.* The basic idea is that everyone is involved in exercising bad judgment. That is a given. The question is not: "Will I exercise bad judgment." I will. I am part of the human race. The only question is how often will I exercise bad judgment; and will I take the proper course of reaction to this inevitable consequence of my humanity.

Going To the Dogs

At age 36, I was given my first command. As commanding officer of LAPD's Pacific Area (Venice Beach to and including L.A.'s Airport) I had the responsibility to lead over 300 officers, detectives and support personnel. This was a great opportunity but also a great challenge and "stretch" for me. I realized that if I were to survive this highly stressful job, I needed the benefits of regular cardiovascular exercise.

Although I eventually grew to enjoy the discipline of the run, I needed some help during those early years. I purchased a Siberian Husky dog and later kept one of her pups. I believe Siberian Huskies make excellent pets; but they do have some negative aspects. Siberians are basically work dogs. They love to pull and run. It's on their genes. I knew this when I selected the breed. My logic went something like this. If Siberians are exercised regularly, they behave and are content. If they are not exercised, they can expend their energy doing bad things. Therefore they can help me maintain the consistency of my cardiovascular program. They can more or less force me to maintain my discipline. Many mornings I would have slept that extra hour had it not been for them.

One morning at "O dark thirty" (an LAPD term for the time just before sunrise) my alarm clock cut my much needed sleep short. I had been on a "call out" the night before. My hours in bed had been few. I somehow made it out of bed, and bounced off the walls of the hall to the utility room, containing our washer/dryer set up. It was avocado season and I had the dogs in that room to keep them from getting into fights with coyotes seeking an avocado dinner.

I would have stayed in bed except for the dogs. I was sleepy. My eyes were not completely open. My head was down. I opened the door and stumbled into the room - right into an open cabinet door. The sharp bottom edge of the door dug into my scalp. My knees buckled. The pain was intense. Blood spurted down my forehead into my eyes. I let out a sharp groan - the result of pain mixed with anger. What happened over the next few seconds was revealing.

While my bellow was still reverberating off the walls, my hands were shooting upward toward the door. My intent was to rip it from its hinges! The door had wounded me. I would retaliate. I was moving laterally into the horizontal process of "blame." I was not rising vertically to the position on the chart of "experience." I was a victim.

As my hands moved toward their goal, my mind was functioning somewhat normally on a parallel tract. I realized that if I destroyed the door, I would have to repair it. I did not want to do that. I stopped in time. But I did not abandon my desire to "blame." As my hands were still in the air, I screamed "Carlson." Ted Carlson had recently painted the cabinets over the washer and had left the doors open. **He** was the culprit. But almost immediately, I realized that painters are supposed to leave painted doors open so they can dry properly. I needed someone, something else to blame.

I shouted "Esther" - that's my wife's name. I decided she was to blame for not telling me that the painter had left open the cabinet doors. Simultaneously she was responding to my initial groan of pain. "Bob," she spoke with compassion, "what happened? Are you O.K.?" The way she said it made me ashamed that I was turning my anger in her direction. I decided she was innocent. But I did not stop the blaming process. For a moment I intended to punish the dogs. My perverted logic was that the whole incident would not have happened was it not for the dogs being in the room. *They* were the cause of my pain. What foolishness!

I had tried to blame an inanimate piece of wood. That didn't "wash." I tried to blame a painter for doing his job correctly. When that failed, I turned my wrath on my wife, who had absolutely nothing to do with the incident. But, I rationalized, she should have warned me. Then I turned my frustration toward my loyal pets who were confused and probably wondering what had gotten into me.

Blame or Grow

Sadly, this is a true story. I have gone through this public embarrassment to illustrate a point. It is difficult to accept responsibility for ones own foolish acts or decisions. The natural instinct is to blame someone -- something else. But until one accepts responsibility for bad judgment, one does not move vertically to truly "experience" the event and move upward toward good judgment.

Often when something goes wrong, when a bad decision has been made, there is some shared responsibility. It is in these situations that I have experienced the most difficulty in identifying and accepting my responsibility. My tendency is to recognize the culpability of others rather easily and ignore my own. Rarely, if ever, does responsibility fall one hundred percent on one person when things go wrong. It is typically a result of a series of events and collective or joint accountability.

I have found it helpful to my own process of pursuing wisdom to search for my responsibility. Even in those cases when the initial facts seem to legitimately point toward someone else, a careful examination will often reveal some culpability on my part. Initially I usually classify my portion of the guilt minimally. Realistically, it is higher than my first estimate would indicate. However, even if my responsibility is slight I can benefit from accepting that responsibility - experiencing the bad judgment and moving toward good judgment.

For example, let's assume a decision by a superior proves faulty and dysfunctional to your efforts and the organization. It is easy and natural to blame the bad decision on your superior. The culpability seems very clear. The Boss made a bad decision. But even in this type of situation one must ask questions like: "Did I provide all of the information that I possessed to help in the decision making process?" "Did I have the courage to disagree, in a respectful way, and explain my position adequately?"

Rarely, if ever, does a one hundred percent to zero ratio exist on the scale that accurately assesses blame. It may be a 60/40, a 50/50, or a 95/5 ratio; but usually there is some joint or collective responsibility. The ethic or character trait of *humility* allows someone to see this concept clearly, accept responsibility and become more effective as a leader. *Humility* makes it possible for one to learn from his/her own mistakes. This is a powerful process that results in more effective leadership.

Summary

The ethic of humility is a precursor to many of the behaviors that are necessary to effective leadership. When this ethic is exercised, the leader is provided more insight, more assistance and most importantly, more admiration. Although not widely accepted as such, humility is an ethic necessary for great leadership.

Assessment

Check those items that apply:
- ☐ I give undivided attention to those who seek my counsel.
- ☐ I recognize that those with less experience or skills may have something to contribute.
- ☐ When I experience failure or unrealized goals, I recognize that I have at least some of the responsibility for that failure.
- ☐ I have developed the willingness to admit when I am wrong.

Plan for Success:

- Which of the desirable behaviors identified in Chapter 2 (see page 30), are rooted in humility?
- Identify some of your behaviors that need attention to ensure humility.
- Describe <u>specific actions</u> that you will take within the next 30 days to improve your commitment to humility.

Leadership: The Power of Character

Chapter 11
__Optimism__

Optimism is defined in Webster's dictionary as: *"An inclination to put the most favorable construction upon actions and happenings; or to anticipate the best possible outcome."* [24] This inclination, character trait or ethic is important to successful leadership.

People prefer following someone who demonstrates that they believe the objective can and probably will be met. On the contrary, they are demoralized by a leader who indicates, in even subtle ways, that they doubt the mission can or will be accomplished. It is human nature to avoid or put little effort into something perceived futile or impossible.

Realistic Optimism

Having said that, I must acknowledge a danger in optimism. My view of optimistic leadership does not mean putting a blind eye to obstacles. A leader who denies or ignores real or perceived obstacles can demoralize their followers as well. Effective leaders strike the balance that I call "realistic optimism." With this phrase I mean properly addressing obstacles without becoming consumed by them. I mean acknowledging the obstacles while retaining focus on the objective. I mean maintaining a "can do" attitude while carefully defining and forming a plan to overcome the difficulties inherent in pursuing a goal.

A leader who has *realistic optimism* acknowledges the presence of barriers to goal achievement. In fact he/she seeks them out. This type of person is not afraid to freely admit that there are problems that need to be addressed. They actually develop ways and means to "surface icebergs" rather than

---

[24] *Webster's 7th New Collegiate Dictionary*; (G & C. Merriam Company 1965)

overlook their presence and allow a collision to occur. One of the dangers of icebergs is that nearly ninety percent of the mass lies below the service.

Using Radar

The proper identification of problems or barriers is the first and probably most important step in resolving them. Good leadership engineers "radar" systems to illuminate problems or dilemmas that should be resolved in order to facilitate the work of his/her followers.

It is possible to communicate a faulty message in one's zeal to be optimistic. A constant note of optimism, without reference to any obstacles, can give the impression that the leader is either naive or purposely uninformed about anything that might cause problems to his/her followers. This type of unbalanced optimism can send a message that a leader does not want to know about the presence of problems. Consequently the problems are often unresolved and goal achievement is obstructed.

I found it helpful to remind my followers that I was interested in becoming aware of problems so we could work together in solving them. I had a sign made and framed so I could mount it on the wall in my office. I had it positioned behind my back, so that people talking with me would have it in plain view. It said in large bold letters: "**Bad news welcome here**." This sign gave my co-workers "permission" to give me negative feedback or make me aware of difficulties they were facing. Often they would refer to this sign prior to relating facts that I needed to know.

I was fortunate to have a great role model to demonstrate the important balance of being a "realistic optimist." Tom Janes, my Commanding Officer in Accident Investigation Division, was a great example. During my tour of duty in that portion of the Department, the whole issue of "Driving Under the Influence" (DUI) became a focus of attention. The social revolution of the sixties expanded drug abuse. Traffic accidents involving the use of alcohol, drugs or a combination of both increased. Over 500 people a week, nation-wide, were being killed in accidents where alcohol and/or drugs were a factor. The laws addressing this problem changed significantly. The legislature and the courts progressively made more demands upon the police. Technology changed. Blood alcohol testing became mandatory. A more sophisticated method of screening for the presence of drugs was needed.

Captain Tom Janes was always optimistic about adapting successfully to change. When additional documentation of DUI arrests became necessary, he freely admitted the hurdles we had to negotiate. When legislation was enacted requiring the submission to a test for blood alcohol levels, he was candid about the problems involved in making the technology change.

Expecting the Best

When the development of a plan to implement testing for blood alcohol was upon us, he said something like this: "There is no doubt that we must begin testing all DUI arrestees for blood alcohol levels. There is also no doubt that there are, and will be, many problems to confront in order to make this change. The technology must be determined. We must budget for, and purchase the necessary equipment. We must prepare and implement a massive training program. There will be many challenges. It will not be easy. But I have every confidence that working together we shall make the transition successfully. In fact, I fully expect other law enforcement agencies to follow our lead as we develop a model program. The process will be difficult; but it will be fun. I believe in you. I love a challenge. This is a great challenge. We will accept it and we will triumph."

Tom Janes was a master at instilling confidence in his leadership team. He always expected the best from us. That was a great encouragement to my colleagues and me. It was hard to disappoint someone who had such high expectations. This is another way to implement the balance of "realistic optimism."

People generally live up to the expectations they sense in their leader. When the perceived expectation is low, then low achievement usually occurs. When the expectation is high, accompanied by all the necessary support, accomplishments are generally at a high level. High expectations communicated properly can have a powerful influence on peoples' attitudes and behaviors.

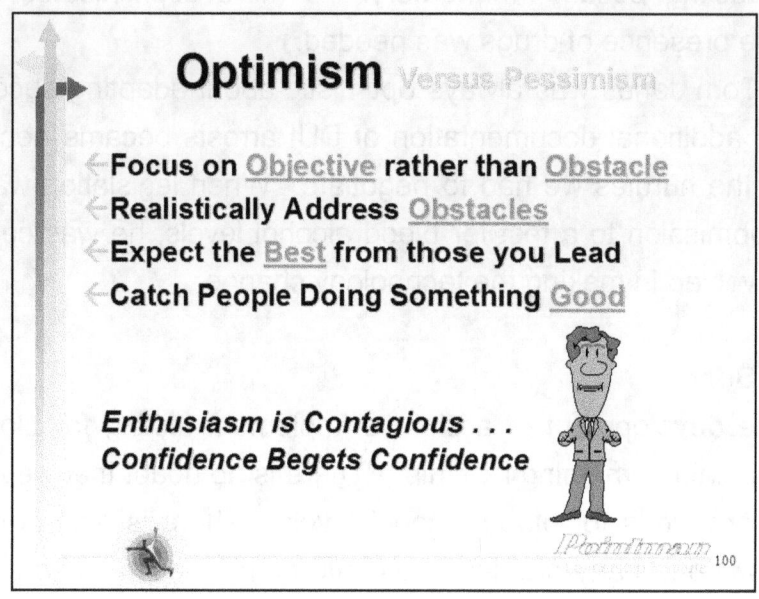

Figure 10

Aborting a Gang Fight

Early in my career, I was interested in supplementing my regular salaried income with so-called "off duty" security jobs. The police department controlled these jobs. An officer could not work unless a work permit was granted. Permits were not granted where a possible conflict of interest existed. For example, an officer could not work in a business supervised or regulated by the police department as in pawnshops, arcades or locations where the primary business was the sale of alcoholic beverages. It was difficult for me to get the opportunity to work these jobs since more senior officers would get first priority.

One morning at "roll call" the Sergeant asked who would be interested in working security at the basket ball game between Lincoln and Franklin High Schools. I should have figured something was wrong when I was the only officer raising my hand. I met with the Sergeant after "roll call" and he gave me the specifics about the job and the necessary forms to complete.

I asked my training officer, Nick Najera, why no other officers were interested in the job. He related that the schools had a low security budget and would only hire one officer for athletic events. He said that the two schools were bitter rivals and that regardless of who won there was usually a fight after the game. He cautioned me of certain aspects about the job and then offered some good advice.

"The gang that is the most dangerous at Lincoln is 'Clover.' You know most of the guys from 'Clover.' Many of them are in the flag football team we coach on Saturdays; and part of the group we have taken to Rams football games," Nick related.

I remembered the hassle we had with the young "gang bangers" at the Rams games. We could not leave them out of our sight. One of us would even accompany a group needing to visit the men's room for fear that they would rob someone in the process.

He told me "Clover" would be at the game and that if a fight occurred, they would be involved. He suggested I meet with them before the game and ask for their help if a fight erupted - to get a commitment from them. I was amazed and confused with his suggestion. How could I get them to help if they were going to be involved? Nick explained that was exactly the point. If they committed to helping me, it would be difficult for them to start anything.

Later at the game, I did just that. I saw the group from the Clover Street Gang hanging together. I approached Manuel, the obvious leader.

"Hi Manuel, -- guys--, 'Que. paso'?"

"Nothing happening 'Rookie'."

"Listen, I may need your help today. I hear there's going to be a "rumble" after the game."

Manuel grinned, "Yeah man, it usually happens."

Now I pulled in a marker. "I know I can count on you men. You won't let your coach down, will you?"

"What do you want us to do?" one of the younger guys asked.

"Look," I leaned in closer to them and whispered, "If a fight starts, I am going to have to handle it myself. I need your help. If I blow my police whistle . . . come running."

Richard, another of the "midgets" (younger members) asked, "You mean we can fight legal?"

"If I blow my whistle, asking for your help, it will be legal - - you can count on it!"

They all began pressing Manuel, "Yeah man, let's do it Manuel. Let's be, like, deputies. Let's help him."

Manuel wasn't real hot on the idea, but he didn't have a lot of choice. Most of them were anxious to jump in.

"O.K. Rookie. You blow on the whistle and we'll be there."

Of course, the fight never happened. With "Clover" committed to helping me stop it, how could it happen? Nick was right. Even "gang bangers" can live up to high expectations.

Making Audits Desirable

Optimism should be seen across a broad spectrum of management activities -- even the traditional negative ones. Take the whole issue of inspections to ensure quality or prevent undesirable conduct. Most employees dislike management audits or inspections. They usually dislike them because on most occasions they have one objective -- to discover something wrong.

Good leaders do not assume that everyone is following policy. An ancient proverb states: "*He who gives an answer before he hears, It is folly and shame to him.*" [25] Another states: "*The naive believes everything, but the prudent man considers his steps.*" [26] An essential part of effective leadership is to set up a variety of systems to provide factual information on what is actually occurring in

---

[25] *The New American Standard Bible*: (Foundation Press, La Habra, CA. 1960) Proverbs 18:13

[26] *The New American Standard Bible*: (Foundation Press, La Habra, CA. 1960) Proverbs 14:15

the day to day operations of any enterprise. Inspections and audits are two methods to provide these types of facts.

On-site inspections are usually structured to identify deficient performance or defective product. That is a legitimate purpose for this management responsibility. An optimistic leader uses audits and inspections as tools to allow positive reinforcement as well. I remember reading a book where the author encouraged leaders to try to "catch people doing things right." Realistic optimists do just that.

One way I put this into practice was to form a policy for inspections.

> "Inspections and audits have a two-fold purpose: (1) to identify excellent behavior or production and (2) to detect substandard behavior or defective production.
>
> All behavior or production that clearly achieves excellence shall be recognized with specific positive reinforcement commensurate with the level of excellence achieved. In other words, employees or groups of employees shall be commended either verbally or in writing depending on the circumstances.
>
> Deviations from our standards that are of a **minor** nature shall be noted; but specific action identifying the individual shall not be taken. Rather the minor deviations shall be addressed with appropriate training. Appropriate *specific* action shall be taken when **major** deviations are discovered."

Employees can actually welcome inspections and/or audits when they know that this type of policy is practiced. Inspections that are practiced to detect and reward superior performance are encouraging. These inspections are not threatening to most employees when it becomes known that minor mistakes are not used to formally censure them. Most people can accept the reality that major acts of negligence or misconduct are addressed swiftly and severely.

Celebrate Victories

Perhaps the most powerful impact of a realistic optimist is that of spreading confidence and enthusiasm. The celebration of even minor victories or accomplishments is encouraging. When people are encouraged about their work their confidence begins to grow. As confidence expands, a person becomes more innovative and willing to take some risks to become more effective. This can result in an upward spiral that builds upon itself. Enthusiasm is contagious.

Successful people are those who enjoy what they are doing. When work is fun and rewarding, people not only work harder, they work smarter. Work becomes a channel to fulfillment. Work is not just viewed as a means to an end. It can become a favorable end in itself. That is the challenge of leadership -- to make work fun and fulfilling. This mandates a *realistic optimism* on the part of leadership.

Leadership: The Power of Character

Summary:

A spirit of optimism creates an atmosphere that is fertile for the growth of excellence and accomplishment. Leaders will either create this nurturing climate, or one that is confining and discouraging. A leader with realistic optimism does not deny the existence of problems; he/she addresses them with a "can do" attitude. He focuses on the objectives, not the obstacles. He/she expects the best from his/her followers. He/she exudes confidence that they will persevere, they will succeed, and they will be victorious.

Assessment

Check those items that apply:
- My followers feel free to bring problem situations to my attention in matters under my leadership.
- My followers seem to enjoy working together even when confronted with major problems.
- I have established ways to identify excellent behavior in my followers and give recognition to those involved in it.
- My followers usually face difficulties with a "can do" attitude.

Plan for Success:
- Which of the desirable behaviors identified in Chapter 2 (see page 30), are rooted in optimism?
- Identify some of your behaviors that need attention to ensure optimism.
- Describe <u>specific actions</u> that you will take within the next 30 days to improve your commitment to optimism.

Leadership: The Power of Character

Leadership: The Power of Character

Chapter 12
Finding a "Fire in the Belly" – Conviction

The character trait of having strong convictions is another essential element in building a foundation for effective leadership behavior. True leadership involves *inspiring* people to reach their full potential. Inspiration involves penetrating to the very core of a person's being. It means somehow giving them a "fire in the belly." It motivates them to the level of emotion and passion. In order to be able to do this, the leader must be impassioned. The leader must have conviction.

Leading with doubt creates doubt. We all communicate our feelings and our attitudes in many ways. Our words are not the only indication of our thoughts. Often "body language", our tone of voice or facial expression expresses more than we intend. Followers can detect doubt or reservation in a leader. When this occurs, the influence of the leader is diluted. In a sense, doubt in a leader is contagious.

Being Contagious

On the other hand, when leaders communicate with deep conviction, they are very persuasive. Strong conviction is also apparent and is likewise contagious. Conviction gives the leader the confidence to be an example. It gives the assurance to show the way rather than just talk about it.

In his book "Self Renewal," John W. Gardiner states:

> "It should now be apparent why anyone concerned for the continuous renewal of a society must be concerned for the renewal of that society's values and beliefs. Societies are renewed -- if they are renewed at all -- by people who believe in something, care about something, stand for something. What about our own values and beliefs?" [27]

---

[27] John W Gardiner, *Self Renewal*; (Harper & Row, N.Y. 1964) Page 115

Leadership: The Power of Character

In that statement he seems to be making a case for having strong beliefs and a commitment to them if one is to have an impact. I agree with this statement. I believe he is describing conviction. Conviction is the ethic that if we choose to live by it, mandates that we live out our beliefs. It means believing strongly enough to take one's belief to the point of commitment and action.

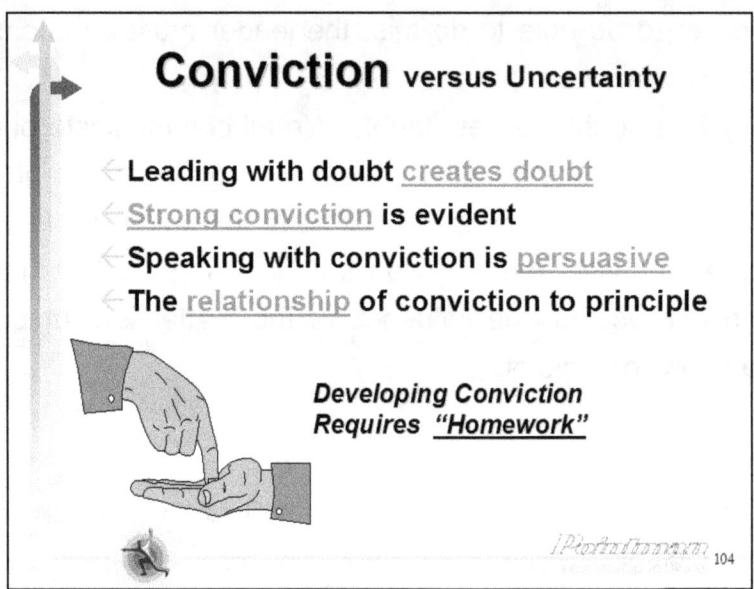

Figure 11

The Big Dipper

Imagine you are a member of a party of pioneers coming across the plains of America during the 1850's. You are now crossing a large desert and have been without water for two days. The temperature is over 115 degrees during the daytime. Therefore, you are traveling at night and trying to sleep under the shade of the wagons during the day. The situation has become critical. People are beginning to die of thirst. To add to the problem the wagon master has admitted he is lost.

It is now 3:00AM in the morning. Suddenly the wagon train approaches a very unique rock formation. An excitement spreads throughout the wagon train because this rock formation is a landmark on the map being used for direction. The map indicates that there are water wells just 3 miles due west of the rock formation. At this point two leaders emerge.

Leader #1 makes a statement something like this: " I know it has been some time since the sun has gone down! We have made several turns to negotiate canyons. We cannot be sure which way is West. I kind'a think west may be over there (He points out into the dark). I am not sure, but I think we should start out in that direction. Why don't we give it a try? If I am wrong we can always come back and start over."

Leader # 2 makes a statement something like this: " Don't listen to him (indicating leader #1). He is wrong. If you will look up at the stars you will notice a constellation right there (He points at a portion of the sky). That group of stars is commonly called 'The Big Dipper.' I have studied celestial navigation. I have acted as a navigator for a shipping company. I know that if you draw a line through the two stars forming the lip of the dipper opposite the handle; that line will point to Polaris. (He points to a star) That is Polaris. Polaris is the North Star. That way is North. There is absolutely no doubt about it. If that way is North then this way (He points ninety degrees to the left) is West. There can be no doubt about it. I am going to get some water. Do any of you want to go with me?"

This story has illustrated conviction. Leader # 2 has it. There is no doubt in his mind. He knows the direction of the wells. He is convinced about the facts. Therefore he has formed conviction and becomes persuasive as he offers leadership.

When there is a vacuum of conviction there will be a crises in leadership. A group or society will flounder when there is no one to call them to a course of action based upon convincing facts or argument. "Where there is no vision, the people perish" is an oft-quoted Scripture that describes the cause of malaise and apathy. In my opinion that is why we are in a leadership crisis. There are few people who have even given serious thought to developing a well-developed belief system. Leadership is based upon opinion polls, financial support, selfish power and "quid pro quo" rather than a strenuous quest for principle, truth and altruistic service.

The Most Feared Danger

It has become vogue to be "open-minded." Some educators have seen this condition as an absolute pre-requisite to learning. They postulate that if a person is to accept information, their mind must be swept free of any absolutes. Dr. Allen Bloom describes this error in his thoughtful book, "The Closing of the American Mind." He explains that the students coming before him had one thing in common -- few or no absolutes. They had been raised in the cult of relativism and taught to fear absolutes.

> " The danger they have been taught to fear from absolutism is not error, but intolerance. Relativism is necessary to openness and this is the virtue -- the only virtue --it is the great insight of our time. The point is not to correct mistakes and really be right, rather it is not to think you are right at all." [28]

He seems to make the point that in the zeal to keep a student open to new thoughts and ideas, some in the education establishment have ironically closed their minds to the possibility that absolute truth may exist. Hence the title of his book.

I believe that our modern culture has discouraged the development of conviction. A person with strong convictions is often described as "narrow minded" or worse yet "judgmental." The irony is that this climate of coerced relativism co-exists with "political correctness." The political correct "police" regularly judge ideas against their own absolutes with inflexible intolerance. This is a strange contradiction.

---

[28] Allen Bloom, *The Closing of the American Mind*.(Simon & Schuster, NY 1987) p 25

Are There Any Absolutes Out There?

I have asked many people about their perception of absolutes. We include this question as part of our seminar. Typically, in countries that have been under the Soviet Union, the answer is "No". In Western countries, including the United States of America, the participants are divided. About half indicate they believe that everything is relative and that no true absolutes exist.

One of the first times that I asked this question in a previous Communist country, all of the participants denied the existence of any absolutes. One man was particularly adamant about his opinion. He seemed incensed that I would even suggest the possibility of absolutes. Suddenly, I had an idea. Perhaps bringing an abstract concept down to the personal level would bring a new perspective. I asked him if he had any children. He responded that he had one child – an eleven-year-old daughter. Then I developed a hypothetical scenario.

"Sir, imagine that one night some men invaded your home at gunpoint. They bind you and your wife with ropes. Then they rape your eleven year old daughter in your presence".

He was visibly disturbed. But I did not stop there.

"Then they murder your daughter".

With my background of being at the scene of many homicides, I went into some detail about the murder – in hindsight, perhaps too much detail. Before I finished developing the gruesome and perverted scenario he jumped to his feet and began shouting words at me. They must have been very angry words. My translator did not translate them. When he paused for a moment in his rage, I asked him a question.

"Sir, under any circumstances can the act that I described be considered good, right or moral"?

He immediately shouted the words, "No – never!" in his own language.

I said, "Sir, we have just determined that you believe in at least one absolute. I wonder if it is possible that more absolutes may exist in your mind."

The whole group of participants began talking. Their talking became more animated and the volume increased. They were speaking in a language that I did not understand. Soon they were heatedly shouting at one another. I turned to my translator. She stated: "Sir, they are arguing."

I replied, "Yes, Jurga. I can see that. What are they arguing about?"

"Some are saying there are many absolutes. Others are arguing that there are only a few", she replied.

A transformation had taken place. Now, all of them realized they believed in *some* absolutes. The only issues now were the nature and number of them.

I have found this true in every seminar around the world. Once a discussion of absolutes is brought down from the abstract conceptual level to the personal level, people begin to realize that they do have strong feelings about certain issues to the point of classifying them as absolutes. In one country, a Colonel who was loath to admit to having any absolutes reluctantly stated, "Well – yes, perhaps I believe in a few absolutes, but only in the area of morality."

Standing Alone

A person who has strong convictions and is willing to be transparent about them runs the risk of confrontation, rejection and criticism. Often a person with strong conviction must "stand alone." In the short term it is safer to go along with the crowd, to compromise one's position on an issue in order to avoid "sticking out." That is why many people find themselves either doing something they would rather not do or agreeing with a position that they inwardly oppose. Rather than lead, they follow. There are certain risks that attach to developing strong convictions.

The Real You

Having said all that, it seems obvious that there is a broad spectrum upon which we all must place ourselves. At one end of the spectrum are those who have little or no conviction about any subject. On the other end of the spectrum are those who have strong convictions about many subjects. The location one occupies on that spectrum, in many ways, defines the essence of their character.

All of us have some absolutes. We all have issues where we "draw the line" and refuse to step across that point. In many ways a person's absolutes are the core of their character. The type of clothes a person wears, the type of car they drive, the way they groom themselves, their choice of music, are all factors that signal to others certain aspects of their nature. However, it is my opinion that one's absolutes reveal more of the true sum and substance of a person's character than all other considerations. A person's absolutes constitute the bedrock of their thinking. Their convictions describe their inner self – their very soul.

Doing the Work to Achieve Conviction

Conviction requires "homework." Conviction does not just happen. Conviction is usually based upon thought, logic or an accumulation of facts. The more examination of available facts, insights and observations on a given subject, the more possible it becomes to develop conviction on that subject. Also, the more your conviction is based upon factual analysis, correct data and logic, the more convincing you are to others.

To build conviction, first gather information. For example, I encourage police officers taking promotional examinations to read professional journals on relevant topics. One practical way to do this is to go through the table of contents of the last two years of police magazines and periodicals. Record the titles of the articles. Then identify from these titles the subjects that are repeatedly addressed. There will usually be four or five topics that fit this profile. Then read each article dealing with the top five subjects. Discuss these issues with respected colleagues. Based upon this research, form your own opinions and conclusions. Finally, sit down and write yourself an essay on each subject. Understand why you believe what you believe.

Take a Stand

Conviction is a result of diligent work, but exposure to information is not enough. One must also have the desire to develop conviction. A person with strong convictions has at some point decided they want to fully understand an issue, they want to see it clearly, and they want to take a stand. There must be an inward desire to be sure about something. Conviction is the fruit of that kind of mind-set coupled with the research and experience to make it possible

> *"Make your ear attentive to wisdom, incline your heart to understanding; For if you cry for discernment, lift your voice for understanding; If you seek her as silver, and search for her as for hidden treasures; Then you will discern the fear of the Lord, and discover the knowledge of God."* The Book of Proverbs, Circa *985 BC* [29]

It is possible to be exposed to much information about a certain topic but still have little or no conviction about that subject. Naturally age and experience are factors that have some bearing on this process; but there are other barriers that impede the development of conviction. For example, a person who has a strong desire to please others at any cost will have difficulty developing conviction. This type of person may be so motivated by either acceptance or approval that they abandon the pursuit of truth. They also ultimately give up the right to lead.

Count the Cost

If you aspire to lead, you must count the cost. To be effective, you must develop conviction on the issues relevant to your leadership. Yet a person with a strong sense of absolutes will be confronted, ridiculed and criticized. Leadership does have a price but it also has great rewards.

---

[29] The New American Standard Bible, (Foundation Press, La Habra, CA. 1960) Proverbs 3:2-5

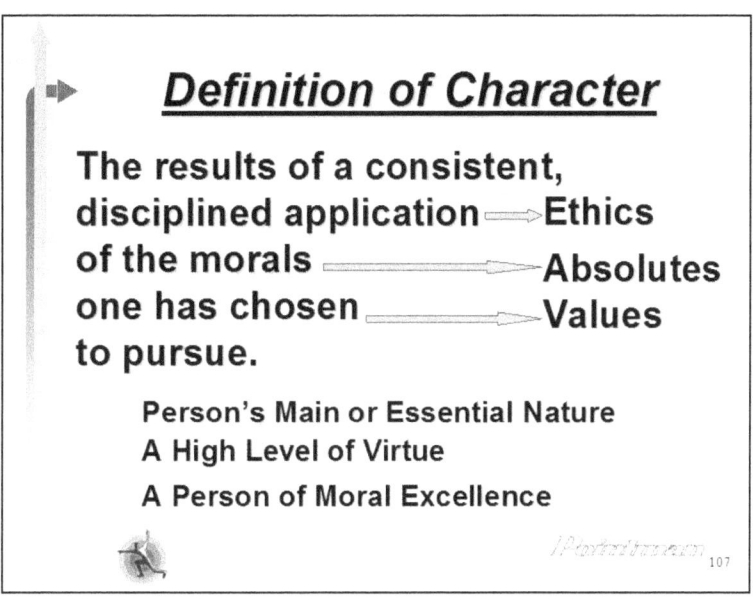

Figure 12

Defining Character

We have completed examining eight ethics or character traits that I believe form a firm foundation for effective leadership behavior. Now that we have done that, we are ready to define character and it's various components. Three words – ethics, absolutes and values – are associated with the idea of character. Often they are inappropriately used interchangeably. I believe they are separate issues. In my opinion all of them have a place in helping us understand character. In Figure 12, I have placed these three words graphically within the definition that I prefer for the concept of character.

> **Character:** *The results of a consistent disciplined application (ethics) of the morals (absolutes), one has chosen (values) to pursue.*

In this definition I suggest that one's ethics are the *application* aspect of his/her character. In other words, one's ethics describe the behavior that reveals their absolutes or morals. As I illustrated earlier in this chapter, everyone has some absolutes. Often they are at the subconscious level. I am suggesting that if one aspires to leadership these absolutes must be identified, developed and consciously pursued. Here is where the notion of values comes into play.

The phrase "values clarification" is used to describe classes or curriculum that help develop personal ethics. Often these discussions are based upon the assumption that no actual moral absolutes exist. It is assumed that everyone must develop their own morality based upon what they value.

I am suggesting a subtle, yet very significantly different approach. Undoubtedly values ***do*** play an important part in defining an individual's character. My definition of character recognized that fact. I am inserting the idea that moral absolutes actually exist. Whether we choose to value them or not, does help in defining our character. This choice, however, does not alter or negate their existence. In other words, my discovery of, and choice to value certain absolutes and deny or devalue others does not alter or change their existence. My position on absolutes does however reveal my awareness of them; and my choice of which to value helps define my character. Later we will examine a few moral absolutes that have been recognized by many civilizations for thousands of years.

Leadership: The Power of Character

Summary

True leaders inspire those being led. In order to inspire, *they* must be inspired. They must really believe in what they are asking others to do. They believe strongly enough to take their belief to the point of commitment and action. Conviction gives the leader the confidence to be an example and the assurance to show the way rather than just talk about it. The "bad news" is that conviction does not typically occur in a vacuum of facts. It develops as a person accumulates facts about the subject at hand. In other words, conviction requires determination and hard work.

Effective leaders do the "homework" to define their character with some strongly held absolutes. They defy criticism, ridicule and rejection while taking a stand. They have conviction.

Assessment

Check those items that apply:

- ❑ I have identified a set of absolutes that allow me to clearly "draw the line" on matters involved in my leadership.
- ❑ I have identified several subject areas that are relevant to my desire to lead and have done the research to form my "belief system" in those areas.

Plan for success:

- Where do you "draw the line." Identify some of your absolutes, professionally and personally.
- Identify at least five subjects that are pertinent to your profession or enterprise. Do the research on these subjects. Write an essay on each of these subjects based upon your research and independent personal evaluation. This will result in the development of conviction.
- Which of the desirable behaviors identified in Chapter 2 (see page 30), are rooted in conviction?
- Identify some of your behaviors that need attention to ensure conviction.
- Describe <u>specific actions</u> that you will take within the next 30 days to improve your commitment to conviction.

Leadership: The Power of Character

Part 3
Principles in an Organization

Chapter 13
Principle Based Leadership

So far I have focused on the application of ethics and character traits to the individual leader. Now I will shift the focus on the organization.

We have briefly discussed the notion of leading effectively through the use of foundational principles. In the previous chapter on "conviction" I emphasized the importance of having firm beliefs (or basic principles) that enable one to speak with conviction. In the chapter on "loyalty", I highlighted the importance of differentiating principle from preference. In this part of the book I will specifically address the importance of principles to leadership and illustrate this importance through a case study.

The use of principles in leadership has many benefits. Principles explain the "why" behind specific directions from the leader. Well published principles give followers broad boundaries within which they can operate. This gives followers the power to apply their expertise and creativity rather than just blindly obey orders. They offer guidance when there are no specific directions or procedures specified for a given situation and the leader is not available. Shared principles are powerful tools in leadership.

In the context of this book, I have chosen the following definition of ***principle:*** A broad statement of truth

Releasing Latent Power

Leaders who emphasize principles give their followers the status of a fellow or colleague. Taking the time and effort to share the conceptual basis that forms the foundation of the enterprise is a not too subtle compliment to those being led. The followers are brought in on the motives, purposes, values and ethics of the leader.

Moreover, the use of principles makes it possible to empower those being led. A clear understanding of foundational principles enables individuals at every level of the organization to innovate the details of how to translate them into strategies, procedures and actions. This creates a strong synergism. People working together with a commitment to the same principles stimulate one another. The dynamic of a myriad of people with diverse skills, backgrounds, interests and experiences coordinating their efforts toward a common purpose is powerful. Without the principles linking them together, the efforts can be disjointed, conflicting and even "off target."

A Model of Principled Leadership

Chief Superintendent John Slater from the London Metropolitan Police has been a valued colleague and team member as we present police leadership seminars worldwide. He uses the chart in Figure 14 to illustrate the relationship of principles to the decision making process as well as the implementation of tactics at the operational level.

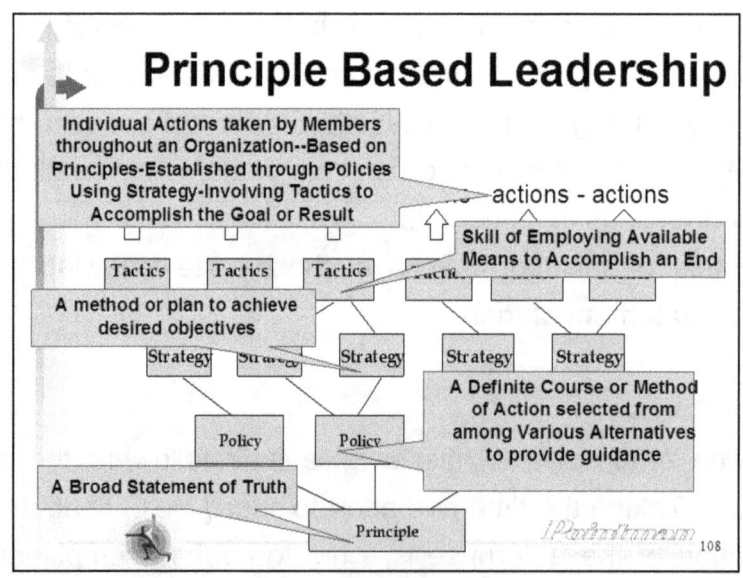

Figure 13

The chart in Figure 13 diagrams the relationship of a few basic principles to actions at the operating level of any organization. We have shown one principle for illustrative purposes. Actually, in most organizations there will be several. Chief of Police Edward Davis documented twenty principles in his leadership of the Los Angeles Police Department.

Several policies may flow from each principle. Likewise there is usually more than one strategy that flows from each policy. The same holds true with tactics. The diagram is limited in numbers to simplify and facilitate the illustration.

In addition to the benefits already discussed, this model of leadership promotes the coordination of many tactics and strategies. Diverse actions at the operating level always have the potential of being competitive, compartmentalized and even in conflict. By being connected or linked together in the same tactic or strategy these potential problems can be reduced or eliminated. Likewise, different strategies that are linked by an underlying principle will also compliment and supplement one another rather than create disunity. Revising, updating or eliminating strategies or tactics are possible if the underlying principle is understood.

Moving from principle to action at the operating level is illustrated by the following examples:

Principle 1: A police department in a free democracy must have the approbation of the community it serves, in order to be effective in accomplishing it's mission of public safety. *This is a broad statement of truth that may imply, but does not demand or specify any action.*

Policy 1.1: It is the policy of Metropolitan Police Department that each precinct Commanding Officer shall establish a "Team Partnership" relationship between the officers of his/her command and the residents of the precinct. *This policy statement begins to move the principle to some type of* *implementation. Policy statements are intended to give guidance, but differ from rules in allowing some flexibility and initiative.*

Strategy 1.1.1: Community Based Policing, a strategy to build a partnership between community members and the officers serving that community, shall be employed. *Strategies narrow the focus of the implementation process. A strategy is intended to build a framework for implementing a policy. It includes specific methods to achieve a desired objective.*

Tactic 1.1.1.1: Upon becoming aware of a pattern of specific crimes in a given community, the involved uniformed patrol officers shall enlist the assistance of recent crime victims in the involved area in organizing a neighborhood meeting. The meeting shall have as it's objective the mobilizing of the residents of the involved area in crime prevention, suspect identification, and when possible, the apprehension and prosecution of offenders. This tactic is based upon the premise that recent crime victims will be motivated to assist officers in these mobilization efforts. *Tactics now focus on specific jobs or tasks necessary to implement the desired strategy.*

Tactic 1.1.1.2: Each team of officers manning a neighborhood patrol car shall conduct monthly public meetings in their assigned areas. Officers shall have the responsibility of planning, arranging for logistics and a meeting facility, selecting the topic, advertising, and presenting a well organized program for these meetings.

Business Example

Principle 2: Satisfied customers tend to become repeat customers. *Once again, this is a broad statement of truth that may imply, but does not demand or specify any action.*

Policy 2.1: Employees at all levels of the organization should be empowered to take reasonable action to achieve a high level of customer satisfaction. *This policy statement is intended to move the "broad statement of truth" to some type of action. The operative word is guidance.*

Strategy 2.1.1: This company shall employ a strategy of willingly accepting our products being returned by unsatisfied customers. The item shall either be replaced or money refunded in order to satisfy the customer. *This strategy is intended to build a framework for implementing the above policy. Typically, a strategy includes specific methods to achieve a desired objective.*

Tactic 2.1.1.1: Train all employees in the specific procedures necessary to appropriately accept returned items. *Tactics emphasize the skill of employing available means to accomplish an end. In this illustration direction is given to prepare employees to apply their skill to the strategy.*

Actions: 2.1.1.1.1: Employees follow a series of steps to properly implement a return strategy.

These examples illustrate how a time-tested principle - an absolute - sets the parameters for policy(s). Policy(s) begins the process of defining specific application of that principle. The policy(s) in turn sets the parameters for strategy. Strategy narrows the focus of alternatives that will implement the policy, leading to tactics. Tactics are manifested at the operating level of the organization in actions. When this paradigm is utilized it is possible for everyone to be "playing from the same sheet of music." It brings unity, coordination and a team spirit.

When top leadership does a good job of defining the first two levels (principles and policies), they empower everyone in the organization to help create, improve and implement strategies and tactics. The more top leadership focuses it's attention on strategies and tactics, the less time and effort it will put into the development and dissemination of the principles and policies. Top leadership must be disciplined enough to first identify and then see that everyone in the organization understands the basic principles and policies of the organization. This is one of leadership's most important responsibilities. I will continue to address this major focus of leadership in Chapter 14.

An Honorable Mission Statement

When I did some work for a major American Corporation in the 1980's, they had a mission statement that embodies four objectives that have given members of this very successful organization direction and motivation: It is:

To honor God in all that we do.

To help our people grow.

To pursue excellence.

To grow profitably.

This mission statement, in my opinion, reflects at least four principles.

1. Work is a vehicle that can demonstrates one's devotion to God.

2. People are the most important resource in any organization, therefore their development must receive a high priority.

3. The achievement of excellence is a worthwhile goal; therefore work should be performed with a strong commitment to diligence and quality.

4. An enterprise will experience healthy growth if it has great motives, values and supports it's people and pursues excellence.

All of the corporation's policies were formed through the grid of these four principles. They combined to forge a firm anchor that brought about stability and yet allowed creative energy and innovation in this very dynamic company. The leaders of this successful organization explained to me that they believe if the first three principles are functioning, they will indeed grow profitably. The history of the company seems to confirm that belief.

The Budapest Challenge

We presented a seminar based upon the material in this book to executive level police officials in Budapest, Hungary. At the beginning of the seminar I presented the four objectives we hoped to accomplish. One of these objectives was: *"To assist the Hungarian National Police to identify a few basic principles (absolutes) upon which their leadership can be based."* One of the participants rose to his feet and stated: "You have told us that you have four objectives. I would like to tell you four things about us. Number one -- Most of us are communists. Number two -- Most of us are atheists. Number three -- There are no *absolutes*. Finally, we do not want to lose our power. Thank you." Than he sat down.

I looked at my colleagues at the back of the room. I suppose I was looking for a play from the "coach" like, "Punt." Actually, I appreciated the candor. At least we were informed! After regaining my composure, I began the seminar. Over the next three days we went through all of the material with encouraging participation by those is attendance. They extended every courtesy and helped us immensely in the application steps.

On the last day, we were discussing the model illustrated in Figure 14 (Principle Based Leadership diagram). The participants readily acknowledged that changes at the *action level* occurred frequently; that flexibility by operating personnel was necessary and desirable within the parameters of established tactics. When asked about changes at the *tactic level*, they explained that tactics change less frequently and appropriately so. When the discussion focused at the *strategy level* they articulated a consensus that proven strategies should remain intact unless justifiable reasons exist for an adjustment or new approach. As we moved down the chart a pattern was developing. Less change seemed desirable or appropriate at each lower level as we approached the foundation of principle. They agreed that established policies should rarely be changed; and then only for very compelling reasons.

When we shifted our attention to the bottom of the chart, I must admit I was a bit apprehensive. I realized that I must confront the issue of principle. Yet, I remembered the emphatic statement of resistance to the notion of absolutes. I asked the question: "What about the issue of principle -- can they be relative in this model of leadership or must they be absolute?" The class responded in unison. I quickly moved my earphones to my ears to hear the English translation. The translator said, "Absolute - the class says the principles must be absolute." I turned to the man who had stood on the first day proclaiming they did not believe in absolutes. I asked him, "Do you agree?" He nodded his head and spoke the Hungarian word indicating affirmation.

Summary

Principle based leadership is a powerful model for the achievement of excellence. Leadership based upon shared principles gives followers broad boundaries within which they can operate. It offers guidance when there are no specific directions or procedures available. Principles can stimulate followers and release them from routine and even obedient behavior to dynamic participation in the constant innovation required for sustained growth and excellence. Leadership based upon principles generates, sets parameters, and coordinates policies, strategies, tactics and eventually behavior by team members. Principles create a firm foundation for organizational integrity.

Assessment

Check those items that apply:
- I (or "we" in the case of an organization) have identified a few basic principles upon which I (we) base my leadership.
- I (we) have clearly articulated and disseminated a few policies connected to each of these principles.
- I (we) have invited our followers to help develop strategies and tactics based upon the articulated policies.

Plan for success:

- Describe at least three benefits of leadership based upon a foundation of principles.
- Develop a plan for Principle Based Leadership in your personal situation. Who should you consult with in this process?

Describe <u>specific actions</u> that you will take within the next 30 days to improve your commitment to Principle Based Leadership.

In the next chapter we will examine the application of Principle Based Leadership in two historical settings.

Leadership: The Power of Character

Chapter 14
Organizational Life Cycle

It seems that organizational entities, like organisms, have a life cycle. Human beings experience the life cycle of (1) infancy; (2) childhood; (3) adolescence; (4) young adult; (5) middle age; and finally (6) old age and death. Plants experience similar successive periods of adaptation, growth and decline. I believe nations, companies, and all other organizations also go though periods of change as they develop, mature and decline.

One perspective of organizational development is depicted in Figure 14. This viewpoint divides the life of organizations that achieve a measure of excellence into four basic periods. The first period I have chosen to call the **vision** of excellence. This is followed by the **struggle** to excellence. The **achievement** of excellence is the pinnacle of the life of the entity. Sadly, this is usually followed by the **decline** of excellence. I believe that this basic model can be applied to most companies, athletic teams, service organizations and indeed even countries.

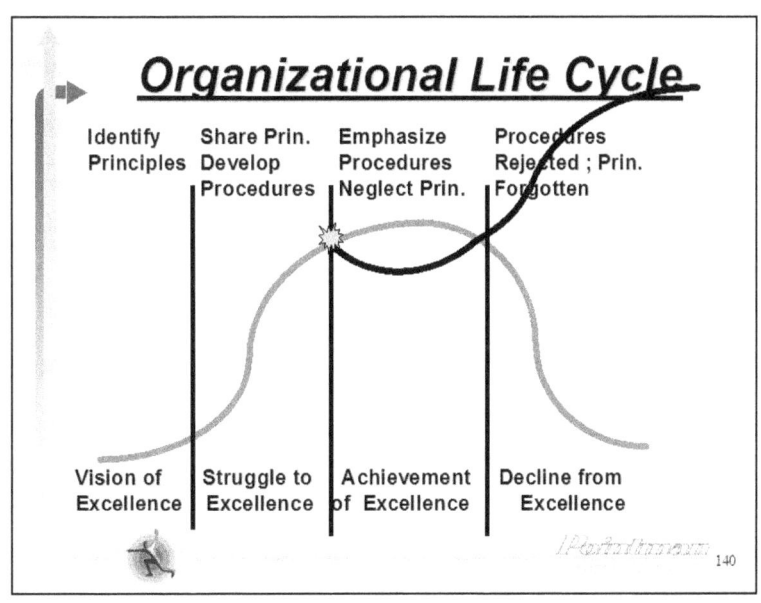

Figure 14
1. The Vision of Excellence:

Organizations that achieve excellence begin with a dream or concept in the mind of an individual or the collective minds of several persons. At some point, someone envisions an ideal; or a group "brainstorms" a notion about greatness. Excellence begins as an idea.

This initial step of conceptualizing can occur in two basic settings: (1) A completely new venture; (2) or an existing entity. Starting a new enterprise will be entrepreneurial in the true sense of the word. From the bedrock of an emerging need someone envisions how to fill that need. Products, an entirely new approach to marketing or providing service may be innovated. In the second setting a new approach may be applied to an existing organization or venture. In other words a mature or dying enterprise may be "reborn" through an infusion of new methods, technology or a new philosophy. In all cases a new idea or set of ideas are envisioned for application.

Inspiration or Hard Work?

Although the initial idea(s) may come suddenly, almost by inspiration, invariably this step of envisioning excellence involves hard work. Ideas must be transformed into practical application. There are many of us who have ideas -- good ideas. But the development of those ideas into reality is another thing. Taking a good idea through the various stages of augmentation required to form a workable plan requires toil and even drudgery.

During this first phase of organizational development certain key principles are identified. The vision must be communicated to others. Therefore, it should be encoded into understandable terms. Those leaders most successful with this step, translate the ideas into principles. Typically, a few principles are identified that must be understood and adopted in order to achieve excellence. The importance of identifying principles cannot be overstated. Leaping from a basic idea directly to methodology or procedures skips a significant process. The identification of principle becomes very useful in the following steps in the struggle to excellence.

The LAPD - A Case Study

Organizations that last over long periods of time may go through several life cycles. In the case of the LAPD the most recent cycle of organizational development began in the decade of 1930 to 1940.

Corruption in the 30's

In the 1930s, the government of the city of Los Angeles became very corrupt. Bribes, political payoffs and criminal influence were commonplace. Corruption extended into the police department. "Bag" men in the police department picked up the graft moneys. Dishonest police officers who wanted to cheat could purchase a copy of the civil service promotional examinations, including the answers, for a price. Morale in the police department was low, especially among the honest men and women who would not "play the game." Actually, there was a sizable percentage of the police who were honest - perhaps a majority. But when corruption extends to the highest levels, the influence of honest people is limited.

The corruption in Los Angeles became so blatant and pervasive that the public became disgusted. They would tolerate it no more. A citizen committee for government reform was formed named C.I.V.I.C. One of the leaders of this committee was Clifford Clinton, owner of Clifton's Cafeteria. The purpose of the committee was to stop the corruption, kick out the dishonest leaders and bring about change that would prevent corruption in the future.

The lack of tolerance for corruption by the citizenry of Los Angeles was a significant condition. This rejection of unethical leadership was absolutely essential to the reform movement that followed. This is always the case. In a free republic, people have the government they deserve. If most of the people acquiesce to dishonest leadership, it will continue and flourish. Cities, states and nations with corrupt leadership have it because the people allow it to continue. Those jurisdictions that enjoy clean, honest government do so because the people demand it. As with most things in life with value, there is a price to pay.

It is dangerous when corruption is pervasive in government. Clinton's family home was bombed. His son Donald Clinton vividly remembers that night and recounted those frightful events to me. But his leadership was courageous. He persevered. He would not give up.

As the saying goes: "The apple does not fall from the tree." Several decades later, the son of Clifford Clinton, Donald, became the chairman of the committee to defeat proposition "F" in 1992. Unfortunately this proposition passed and sadly, returned Los Angeles to a system with political control of the police department, much as it was in the 30's. Curiously, history seems to repeat itself when people are not vigilant.

"Throw Out the Thieves!"

In 1938 a recall election was held. The corrupt regime was ousted and an honest judge named Fletcher Bowron was elected mayor on a reform ticket. One of his first acts was to replace the Chief of Police. A Marine Corps General was appointed on an emergency basis to act as Chief of Police for one year. He had a difficult job and did it well. Officers were fired, disciplined and a few sent to prison. Others who did not relish the changes retired or quit.

A few years later William H. Parker became the Chief of Police. He competed for the position through an objective civil service examination process. Parker was one of a group of honest cops who yearned for a "clean" department. He with men like Harold Sullivan, Frank Walton, Roger Murdock, Richard Simon, Noel Mc Quone and Thad Brown had dreamed of the days when honesty and professionalism could thrive. In the years and months leading up to the recall movement, they had developed a vision of excellence for the Los Angeles Police Department. In this process, principles were identified that would be necessary to adopt for the vision to become a reality. The identification of the necessary principles was a substantial accomplishment.

The Mayflower Compact

A similar set of circumstances occurred during the early beginnings of The United States. People coming to this great land had a dream. The dream was not complete; but it had the essentials for the "cycle of excellence" to begin. Even before the first boats struck shore the "Mayflower Compact" was written. It described their vision of excellence. It was not a comprehensive and exhaustive document of laws, or even a constitution, but it outlined a vision: the congruence of liberty with law.

During those beginning years principles were identified that would be necessary for the next steps. The Federalist Papers many years later specified those principles and philosophies.

2. The Struggle to Excellence

Excellence always involves a struggle. By definition it means to rise above, to surpass. The Latin roots of the word imply the peaking of a hill. A hill is not climbed without effort. There is always commitment and tenacity of purpose involved in excellence. You do not achieve excellence through luck or haphazard efforts.

In this period we have chosen to call "***The Struggle to Excellence***" at least two important things occur. First, the principles identified in **"The *Vision of Excellence"*** *are* communicated. Secondly, based upon the degree the principles are understood and accepted, methods and procedures (strategies and tactics) are developed to translate the principles into action. These are two important developments.

Sharing the Vision

The primary leader or leadership team typically communicate the principles identified in the infancy period of the organizational development. Individuals and teams that fully understand the importance of this function devote ample resources to it. They use diverse and redundant methods to ensure understanding takes place. The successful transfer of the "vision" of excellence to others is absolutely essential. Others will not be motivated participants if they do not see the vision. They definitely will not be inspired contributors in the struggle if they do not fully share the vision. The vision of excellence must be shared by a substantial number of individuals in order for it to become reality.

When the vision is clearly understood, it is more likely that those being led will join the struggle. The more people that choose to join the struggle, the more it becomes possible to generate and implement effective methods and procedures to achieve excellence. The leadership team will not have an exhaustive accumulation of all of the ideas that can contribute toward success in the struggle. As we have said earlier, it is often the people at the first line, or operating level, who have the necessary insight.

The Critical Mass

Progress in the achievement of excellence occurs when a sufficient number of people join in the struggle. In a sense, a "critical mass" is formed. A synergy begins wherein members of the organization stimulate one another. Enthusiasm and excitement begin to build. Individuals begin to contribute their expertise or talent to the enterprise. At this point, methods, procedures and standards are specified that are necessary to the rise to excellence. Procedural manuals may be written, training materials developed or a constitution or bylaws documented. In other words, the ways and means to implement the principles are put into place.

The important dynamic in this phase of organizational development is the participation of the so-called "critical mass." This is why it is so important to translate the core ideas of the vision into principles. It is also why it is so important to communicate these principles to as many people as possible. When people clearly understand the principles and "buy into them", they make important contributions to the implementation process. They offer innovative and often very unique ideas that accelerate the rise to excellence. People throughout the organization participate in the formation of strategies and tactics.

Parker the Preacher

In the case of the LAPD, William H. Parker articulated the principles. During his first few years as Chief of Police he took every opportunity to explain the vision that he and his colleagues had developed. He spoke within the department. He used "roll call" assemblies. He communicated with the public at large, speaking at community and service clubs. He recognized the importance of sharing the vision and he did so in a variety of settings and as often as possible.

Parker was a great communicator. His speeches approached the level of great oratory. He rarely spoke extemporaneously, but rather, used a well-developed text. He used speech writers to assist him polish and fine tune his thoughts. Sergeant Gene Rodenberry, who later went on to create the "Star Trek" series, was one of the more well known writers. Parker placed a high priority on communicating.

His strong commitment to communicating the vision paid off. Within a few years he had won the loyalty and endorsement of a large following. Officers within the organization accepted the validity of his principles. They were inspired by his personal conviction to them. He ignited enthusiastic support from a broad base including elected officials, intellectuals, community leaders and the people at large.

Parker's career path within the police department gave him expertise as a traffic specialist. He was one of the first graduates of the Northwestern University's Traffic Institute. He did not have strong expertise in many other facets of police work. He needed assistance from colleagues in developing the specific methods and procedures (strategies and tactics) to implement the principles. He got their assistance. His efforts to win a strong base of support within and without the department paid off.

Sharing the Vision Pays Off

During Parker's first ten years as Chief, the famous and often plagiarized LAPD Manual was written. A cadre of researchers and writers prepared "Daily Training Bulletins." Other systems to ensure implementation of the principles were developed. All of this was possible because of <u>the effective sharing of the principles</u>. I cannot overemphasize the importance of this action.

The Federalist Papers

One can see a similar application of this model in the development of the American Republic. Three statesmen - Hamilton, Madison and Jay collaborated in the writing of "The Federalist Papers." These essays were written to explain the American "Vision of Excellence." The essays were published in American newspapers under the pseudonym "*Publious*." Their purpose was to build the "critical mass" necessary to move forward in adopting the U.S. Constitution -- the formal structure of our government.

Based upon the effective sharing of the principles in the Federalist Papers, the development of the American Republic moved forward rapidly. In my opinion, never before had the masses of people been included in the formation of a country in such an effective manner. In those early years of our history, a high percentage of the people understood what our government was all about. A large majority of the people endorsed and supported it. They believed in their country because they understood it. They had a good grasp of the principles upon which the government was based. Therefore, many contributed their efforts to its development.

In my opinion this sharing of principles and the formation of a moral consensus was one of the most important factors in forming The United States of America. This consequential process made possible the unparalleled success and rapid rise to excellence Americans have enjoyed.

The Achievement of Excellence

The pinnacle of the life of the organization is also its most dangerous period of time. It is the most fragile. A dangerous shift in priorities or focus of attention generally occurs. Typically, the procedures and methods that accelerated the rise to excellence are emphasized and the principles underlying them are neglected. It is assumed that everyone understands the principles. There seems to be no real need to "rehash" them. The methods leading to excellence are working. Why continue to spend time on the underlying principles?

All the while, new people join the organization. As time passes, those involved in the *struggle to excellence* depart. Soon there are many that are driven by the procedures and methods (strategies and tactics) without an understanding of the principles or policies behind them. This shift in motivation begins deterioration in commitment and enthusiasm.

People begin entering positions of leadership that do not understand the principles or reasons behind the methods and procedures. When their leadership is contested they have difficulty explaining a rationale to support it. When rules, strategies, methods and procedures are challenged, the leaders are unable to defend them adequately.

A Costly Neglect

The neglect of principles leads to other negative implications. Without a firm foundation of principles the maintenance of essential leadership ethics erodes. Integrity, loyalty and all other ethics that support effective leadership behavior are impacted. For example, it is impossible to maintain strong conviction without a belief system rooted in principle. Therefore, leadership begins to fade and the stage is set for the decline from excellence.

In the case of the LAPD, Period #3 - ***The Achievement of Excellence*** began in the decade of the 1950's. By that time, most of the famous LAPD manuals were written. The police academy had worldwide fame, and many police agencies, both American and International, flocked to observe "the new breed" of police officers and scientific police work.

The TV program "*Dragnet*", depicting actual LAPD cases, had a synergistic effect on the Department. Not only did it tell the world about the new Los Angeles Police professionalism; it became the model for young officers like myself to follow. It built a new positive image that gave rise to strong public support. This support led to more financial backing, continued improvements and more effectiveness. Talented people were attracted to join the ranks. In short, a "virtuous cycle" was created.

During the decade of the seventies a shift began to take place. The procedures and methods utilized by the Department were the center focus of

Leadership: The Power of Character

management. The principles began to be neglected. Chief Ed Davis recognized this error and mounted an effort to reemphasize principles. He formed and published "*The Twenty Management Principles of the Los Angeles Police Department.*" A copy of these principles was posted at each of the Department's facilities. They became part of the curriculum of the training at the Police Academy. This action helped diminish the shift in emphasis from principles to methods and procedures. It delayed the normal erosion of Principle based Leadership.

The Cancer of Relativism

In the decade of the eighties a shift in emphasis once again took place. This time, a hostile political environment actually encouraged the abandonment of principle in the administration of the Department. Elected officials, the judiciary and political action groups attacked the Department's emphasis of absolutes. They supported the doctrines of inclusion, pluralism and diversity. Taken to extremes, these noble ideas can result in relativism, the lowering of standards and eventually a deterioration of excellence.

> *"Pluralism offers much in the way of variety, and the enrichment we bring to one another is incalculable. But when pluralism breeds a doctrine of relativism the cost is too great."* [30]

During this decade, the strong political support the Department had enjoyed for over forty years shifted to an adversarial relationship. The Chief of Police was put on the defensive. Much of his attention was diverted to a struggle to maintain necessary standards, equipment and staffing. The leadership of the Department was purposely discouraged and in some cases prohibited from emphasizing absolutes. Consequently, the principles began to erode. Standards

---

[30] Ravi Zacharias, *Deliver us from evil* - page 95

were compromised. The natural tendency to emphasize strategies, methods and procedures (tactics) occurred.

A similar phenomenon seems to have occurred in the United States in general. The ideology and political philosophy that spawned the amazing American culture and nation is largely unknown by most of its citizens. Today few Americans even know what the Federalist Papers are, much less understand their contents. Very few have read or studied them. Rather, there has been a marked departure from the principles that created American greatness.

The Intolerance of the Relativists

As a matter of fact, those who **do** advocate leadership based upon these time-tested principles are rebuffed and rejected. A nominee to the Supreme Court in the late 1980's was viciously attacked and rejected, primarily because he advocated basing court decisions on principle - the original intent of the framers of our constitution. Apparently, the present political climate favors a changing "relative expediency", or "socially active court", rather than adhering to principle.

Our legal institutions seem committed to the god of *process.* No longer does the legal system seem interested in what is "right and just." Rather it is consumed by the notion of adhering to a technical protocol. Although the original rules governing *process* were designed to get to "the truth of the matter", the process has actually become an end in itself. Principles or absolutes are held up to scorn.

To be "politically correct" seems more important than doing right, moral or ethical. It is my opinion that this condition is the by-product of neglecting principle. When one does not understand the principles behind ethical or moral behavior they are more apt to reject them or place less value upon them.

<u>The Decline from Excellence:</u>

The final period in a typical cycle of organizational life is *The Decline From Excellence.* Typically, two significant conditions describe this grievous end to an encounter with excellence: (1) a questioning and eventual rejection of the procedures or methods (strategies and tactics) that led to excellence, because (2) the underlying principles are forgotten.

Excellence always involves high standards and a deep commitment to them. Human nature, such as it is, resists blindly accepting high standards or diligence in work. Rather, we feel compelled to ask the question "why?" People often feel the need to probe the reason they are asked to adhere to a high standard. They must understand the logic behind the necessity of hard work.

If an organization follows the typical pattern outlined above, eventually individuals asking the hard questions relating to the "why" of required behavior do not get suitable answers. Consequently they begin to challenge the requirements and eventually reject them in some manner. At this juncture, since leadership also has lost sight of the rationale behind the requirements, it either joins the rebellion or is unable to successfully resist the floodwaters of rejection and change. Ironically, the behaviors that made the rise to excellence possible are abandoned. Sadly, the organization begins its plunge to mediocrity, ineffectiveness and irrelevance.

The Inevitable is Not Inevitable

The good news is this described pattern of cyclical behavior does not have to occur. There are steps that can be taken to maintain the rise to excellence. Since the basic problem is the neglect and abandonment of principles, the solution is the continued emphasis of them.

The most important step in the process of problem solving is the accurate definition of the problem. Once a problem has been carefully described, the corrective action often becomes obvious. A studious examination of historic evidence relating to the rise and decline of organizations reveals an interesting connection with principle. When the principles that make an organization great are neglected - the organization declines. Organizations that regularly reinforce their principles and demonstrate a strong commitment to them keep the struggle for excellence alive and well. Therefore, an emphasis on principle is the antidote for the normal decay that may seem to be inevitable.

Summary

Organizations that achieve excellence do so because of strong leadership. An individual or group of individuals identifies the principles that will lead them to greatness. These principles are then communicated broadly to secure a "critical mass" of supporters. The "critical mass" develops the specific methods, procedures and technology to begin the rise to excellence. As excellence is achieved, the emphasis upon the principles that made it possible can shift to the procedures and methods. If this dangerous adaptation is allowed to continue, the principles will be neglected and eventually forgotten. The high standards in the methods and procedures will be abandoned. The organization's greatness will decline.

The tragic decline experienced by many great organizations does not have to occur. Principle Based Leadership can be sustained. When the emphasis on principle is maintained and even strengthened, the decline will not occur. The focus on principle will either reaffirm the validity of existing procedures, process and rules; and/or stimulate the generation of updated and more effective strategies and tactics, while maintaining the organizations values.

Action Steps:

- Where is your organization (or family) on the life cycle chart?
- What can you do to help your colleagues and followers understand the "Organization Life Cycle."
- Read the "Federalist Papers" to help you understand principles that helped form The United States of America.
- Develop a plan to ensure that your principles are reinforced during the development of your organization or family.

Describe <u>specific actions</u> that you will take within the next 30 days to improve your commitment to resist the normal deterioration in organizational development.

Leadership: The Power of Character

Chapter 15
Steps of Leadership

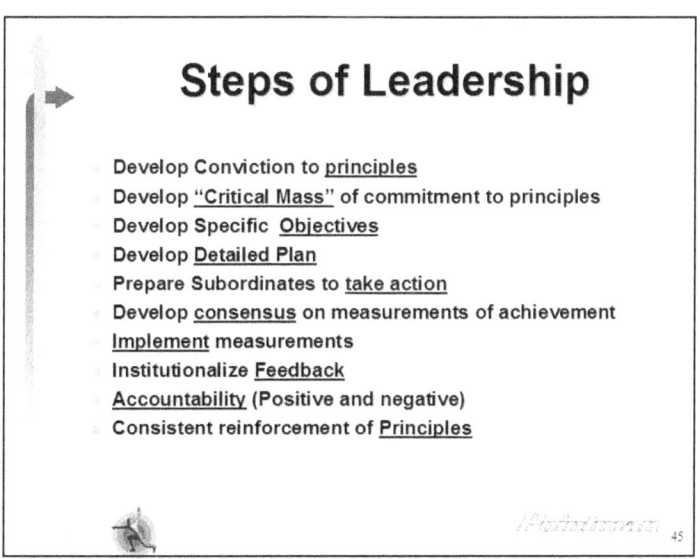

Figure 15

In this book I have emphasized the ethics or character traits that I believe are absolutely necessary to powerful leadership. The focus has been on this basic truth: *Effective leadership must be based upon strong personal ethics and well thought out organizational principles.* Once this truth is understood, embraced and acted upon, it is appropriate to shift our focus to a few practical steps of application. The steps we will examine are the framework for the normal **process** of applied leadership. It is assumed that the foundation of character has been, and continues to be developed.

This chapter will outline the basic steps in the process of leadership. It is not an exhaustive study. Rather, this is intended to present the most common steps one should consider in any leadership situation.

Step #1: Develop Conviction

The first step in leadership is for the development of a strong conviction by the leader (and/or leadership team) in the direction he/she intends to go. This often involves goals, objectives or desired change. As previously stated, the leader must be able to clearly understand and articulate the goal(s). The leader(s) will be most effective in this process if they have developed conviction about their leadership. Conviction is strong when it is based on facts. This means the leader(s) must "do the homework", gather the facts, analyze them and have a logical basis for his/her position.

The identification of a few relevant principles will be very helpful during this first step. You will recall that in the context of this book, I have defined a principle as "*a broad statement of truth.*" When a leader (or leadership team) has identified relevant principles bearing on the issues at hand, the development of conviction will naturally occur.

Let's use as an example a new company that manufactures and markets a high tech product. The leadership team is developing their whole approach to doing business. They must build this new enterprise from the ground up. Their product is a very complex unit utilizing the cutting edge of technology. The product has the potential of radically improving the reliability and safety of a new medical procedure. The leadership has identified several relevant principles. The first one is that *potential buyers of highly complex new technical devices will be more likely to purchase a unit that is backed by a solid guarantee of timely technical support.* This principle (along with other relevant principles) will form the foundation of policies, strategies and tactics in the marketing and servicing of the product. It will also build strong conviction in the leader(s).

Conviction must be based upon facts. Therefore the identification of relevant principles are very important in this first step.

Step #2 Develop a "Critical Mass" of Commitment to the Principles

Once the relevant principles have been identified and the resulting conviction developed, it is time to bring others aboard. This step is particularly relevant in large and medium sized organizations. In a very small enterprise or social unit it may be irrelevant.

I experienced a somewhat humorous reaction to teaching this step to a group of government officials in Bolivia. They wondered why it was important to have a very serious church meeting at this point. Then it hit me. Bolivia is predominately a Roman Catholic culture. When I used the phrase "critical mass", they assumed I was referring to a Mass at the cathedral. Of course I was using the language pertaining to atomic reaction. A critical mass of significant support is also necessary to acquire "buy in" that can result in an "explosion" of broad support by a majority of followers in a leadership situation.

Selection of those forming the "critical mass" is important. The leader(s) should identify those who are most influential. Often the "most influential" do not have formal rank or status. They may be influential due to their unique expertise. They may be part of the "critical mass" because of an unexplained charisma. Or they may just be natural indigenous leaders. Often it is helpful to bring those who are expected to oppose leadership on the issue at hand. If they are exposed to all of the relevant principles, they may either join the supportive team or at least reduce or minimize their resistance. People outside the organization may also be helpful members of the "critical mass." For example, stockholders, important clients or the media can have a role here.

The "critical mass" will also be of great assistance in developing the strategies, tactics and methodology to bring meaningful application of the principles.

Step #3 Develop Specific Objectives

Once a "critical mass" of support for the principles and policies has been developed, it is time to develop some very specific objectives and/or goals. Remember, it is most effective to have a time table for each objective or goal. I believe a goal is incomplete without a reference to time.

For example, I may say that I have a personal goal of reading five books. Later, someone may approach me and ask: "Have you reached your goal of reading those five books?" I can reply: "No, but I am still working on it." It would be better to say: "I have a goal of reading these five books by February 1 (and specify the year)." Then my goal achievement or lack thereof will be measurable. Specific objectives and/or goals are very important in the leadership process.

Step #4 Develop a Detailed Plan

The detailed plan consists of the steps necessary to be able to accomplish the objectives or goals. In other words, the detailed plan is the road map or blueprint to guide the followers to the goal. Thinking back to our diagram of Principle Based Leadership (Figure 13, page 105), these steps will include strategies, tactics and actions.

For example, to achieve the goal of reducing "response time" by police units to emergency calls it may include the specific steps of: (1) organizing a "split force" of response units and general patrol units, (2) educating the public to use "911" for only true emergency situations, (3) responding to non-emergency calls on an appointment basis during off peak hours, (4) formally and publicly eliminating certain non-essential services.

Step #5 Equip Subordinates to Take Action

Followers cannot move toward an objective or work on the detailed plan if they are unable to do so because of a lack of training, equipment or other necessary prerequisites. Giving clear direction is not enough. Even followers who have been inspired may not be able to implement the steps of the plan. They must have the capacity to do what they have been asked to do.

In my opinion, this is one of the most neglected responsibilities of leadership. Many leaders, who do an excellent job of identifying principles, forming policies, setting objectives and specifying action steps, fail at this step. The leader(s) is responsible for giving the followers all they need to do the job.

For example, if you ask a follower to develop a PowerPoint presentation based upon an outline you have developed, you must ensure the follower is prepared for this task. It may be necessary to send them to a class on using the PowerPoint software. Or you may elect to personally mentor or train the follower to utilize the program. Equipping the followers may also mean granting them authority. The leader is responsible to do whatever is necessary to make the assigned task possible.

Step #6 Develop a Consensus on Measurements of Achievement

Most people agree that some method of measuring and evaluating progress toward goals is necessary. However this important step of building a consensus about those measurement is often neglected. This failure can bring about frustration and disgruntlement. Those being measured must accept the measurements as "fair". For example, people will resist being measured in any area over which they feel they do not have control. They will feel it is unfair to be measured and evaluated in an area or function where another entity within the organization has control or great influence.

For example, after setting a goal of reducing response time on "911" emergency requests for service, I unilaterally defined response time and began measuring it. The Chief Officers reporting to me immediately relayed the dismay of the Captains running our 18 police stations. They cried "foul." Our measurement system defined response time as the interval between the initial telephone call to the police and the arrival of the police car at the scene of the event. I defended my position explaining that as far as the individual requesting police service was concerned the time being measured was indeed our "response time."

The Captains argued that our Communications Division, who were charged with accepting and dispatching the request for service via radio transmission, was not under their control. They further explained that often requests for service were delayed during this process for a variety of reasons. They felt it was unfair to be measured and evaluated on a process over which they had no control or influence. They were right. When I admitted my error and adjusted the computer program to measure the time interval between the dispatch of the "call" and the arrival of the units under their command, they were happy. They willingly accepted the accountability system that they deemed "fair."

Step #7 Implement Measurements

Once a consensus is developed on the fairness and appropriate nature of the measurements – implement them. This may seem obvious. I have purposely separated this step out from the others to draw attention to it. Many leaders talk about what the indicators of achievement, or lack thereof, should be. However, for many reasons the actual measurement systems are never designed or actually implemented. This step must be done in order to continue the remaining steps. Basic principle: "Workers do what leaders measure".

Step #8 Institutionalize Feedback

Regular and timely feedback must be provided on goal or objective accomplishments, or lack thereof. Author Warren Bennis talks about the essential leadership responsibility of retaining focus on the "vision" of the enterprise. One of the ways to do this is to provide relevant and understandable information to those doing the work on the results of their efforts.

Think how silly it would be to hang a bed sheet in front of the pins at the end of a bowling alley. The players could still roll the ball down the alley. The ball would pass under the sheet and perhaps strike some of the pins. But the players could not see how many or which pins were hit and which were still standing. They could not evaluate the effectiveness of their first attempt. They could not correctly determine what their next effort should be. That is precisely what occurs when followers are not given timely and understandable information about the effectiveness of their efforts.

Feedback allows the followers to connect their efforts to results. They can assess their effectiveness. They can then make appropriate adjustments or increase their efforts on actions that have been successful.

Step #9 Accountability (positive and negative)

I have purposely positioned "positive" accountability first. By this phrase, I mean the process of encouragement, recognition and reinforcement. Of course, appropriate sanctions or retraining must be included in this "mix" of the leaders reactions to success or failure.

None of the previous steps in this process of leadership will be completely effective unless there are actions by leadership to reinforce them. Studies have shown that followers are more interested in what the leader does than what he/she says. These studies have revealed that followers are especially interested in two actions of the leader. They want to know what the leader (1) rewards, and what he/she (2) sanctions.

Step #10 Consistent Reinforcement of Principles

To complete the loop, there must be a consistent reinforcement of the principles supporting the policies, strategies and tactics (or procedures). In Chapter 13 dealing with "Organizational Life Cycle", I described the normal cycle that ends in "The Decline from Excellence." The way to prevent this entropy from occurring is to regularly revisit the principles that were identified in step #1.

It is very natural to explain the principles and then neglect them. The natural assumption is that everyone will remember and understand the importance of them. This is usually not true. Normal attrition of the work force can result in new members not ever being exposed to the principles. Also, followers who at one time did understand the principles begin to focus on the strategies and other methodology that flowed from the principles. This can result in eventual resistance to the methodology or an inappropriate revision of it.

Summary

In this chapter I have presented a basic process that involves several steps of leadership. It will apply to most leadership situations; but can be revised or expanded depending upon the situation. I have attempted to apply many of the concepts covered in this book. This process integrates the concept of Principle Based Leadership with some traditional management techniques.

Plan for Success

1. What step(s) outlined in this chapter do you want to improve in your leadership style?
2. How does this process relate to the desired leadership behaviors? (figure 1, page 31)
3. Describe the relationship of this process to the eight ethics or character traits. (figure 2, page 38)
4. Which of the 10 steps have you most often neglected?

Chapter 16
Core Beliefs

Principle based leadership can be sustained. It all depends on the convictions or belief systems of the leadership team and most importantly the Chief Executive Officer. These convictions rest upon a foundation of that person's character or ethics.

The character traits of an individual are formed by bedrock of what I choose to call core beliefs. Everyone has a set of core beliefs. These become the basis for one's approach to life and also their ethics or character traits. These core beliefs relate to such primary questions as: Who am I? Where did I come from? Where am I going? What is the purpose of my life? Are there any absolutes? The answer to these and other similar cardinal questions form a person's *worldview*. One's worldview has a powerful influence on his or her character and ethics. First we will focus our attention on the connection between "core beliefs" and ethics.

Many readers will accept the eight ethics or character traits outlined in Part II as functional in achieving effective leadership behavior. They agree that ideally it is desirable for leaders to embrace them. I would like to divide those who accept this premise into two groups.

Ethics Work Better

The first group are those who accept the described ethics based upon *utilitarian* reasons. By this term, I mean those who accept the ethics primarily because they work. Their position is grounded in experience. These people agree that a leader who sincerely adopts the eight ethics will be more likely to consistently practice effective leadership behavior and ultimately become more effective in leading or influencing people.

We presented an "Ethics in Leadership" seminar to over 200 top police leaders in Beijing, China, at the National Police Academy. As part of that seminar we discussed 10 principles for social order derived from the ancient

Hebrews. These are known in the west as "The Ten Commandments." Since we suspected that most of our audience had an atheistic worldview, we gave a secular, practical application of these principles to leadership.

When we came to the principle addressing adultery, my colleague Chief Superintendent John Slater from the United Kingdom asked a question. He said: "Who do your subordinates think you value most? Do they think you value them (the subordinates), or your own family members?" At first they remained silent. He requested them to answer. Through the translator they replied as a group: "Our own family members." John announced that he was not surprised by their answer. Then he asked them a rhetorical question: "If your subordinates become aware that you have betrayed your family through an act of adultery, can they not expect that someday you will betray them." They got the point. The logic of practicing fidelity to solemn vows or commitments in order to win trust as a leader is difficult to refute. This is an example of accepting an ethic for utilitarian reasons.

Morally "Right"

The second group is those who accept the ethics principally because they believe it is "right" to do so. These people not only believe the ethics are functional, they also believe they are virtuous. Their position is grounded in the morality of the ethics. These are people who have a worldview that usually includes purpose and destiny. They see a world of design rather than chance and accident. Their core beliefs often include a "supreme being" or God. They believe that a leader who embraces the ethics will not only be effective, but also moral in doing do so.

Although both groups have features in common, there is an important distinction in those who add the moral/ethical dimension to their reason(s) for acceptance. I have found that those who believe in the innate goodness or "rightness" of a position are more likely to be committed to that position. They are more apt to persevere in clinging to a course of action based upon them.

They are also more apt to change long held practices or opinions if they are convinced that the suggested new ones are "right."

We have observed that there are many pressures in the real world that push leaders toward compromise and expediency. It is easy to fall back to behavior that is dysfunctional to good leadership just to escape the hassle and relentless intimidation that seems to plague leaders. If one accepts the ethics we have discussed solely for practical reasons (they work), they will be more likely to surrender their position if the pressure is great enough. On the other hand, if the notion of morality or "doing what is right" is added to the mix, the leader can be strong in his/her endurance. In other words, those who believe the suggested ethics are moral absolutes will practice them more consistently than those who just believe they are useful to good leadership.

We have already discussed the issue of absolutes in Chapter 11. Accepting the notion of moral absolutes is an important part of a person's core beliefs. Your position on absolutes will thrust you into one of two positions. You either believe in clear concepts of right and wrong, or you believe that morality is relative and subjective.

There is an irony in taking the position that morality is relative. Proclaiming there are no absolutes is taking an absolute position. In a real sense, the question is not if one believes in absolutes or not. Rather it is: "what are your absolutes?" As we illustrated in Chapter 11, when the discussion of absolutes is shifted from the conceptual level to the personal level most people agree they have a place where they draw the line and declare something unacceptable.

Will and Ariel Durant devoted their lives to researching and analyzing history. They wrote many volumes, documenting their research. Their final book, and in my opinion their most important work, is entitled: "The Lessons of History." In that culmination of their brilliant contribution to civilized society they make the following observations:

> A little knowledge of history stresses the variability of moral codes, and concludes that they are negligible because they differ in time and place,

and sometimes contradict each other. A larger knowledge stresses the universality of moral codes, and concludes to their necessity. There is no significant example in history, before our time, of a society successfully maintaining moral life without the aid of religion. [31]

Here the Durants (reportedly agnostics) explained that although it is easy to form the opinion that moral absolutes either do not exist or are unnecessary, just the opposite is the case. Why then have we experienced such an assault on this historically proven social mainstay?

A Hidden Agenda?

The concept of moral and ethical relativity has been preached relentlessly by radical liberals in western civilization during the last several decades. This doctrine became part of the "pop culture" of the sixties. Could it be that many people in our public institutions promote this religion unashamedly to advance their personal political agenda? Could they have a vested interest? For example, is it not true that the trashing of the traditional moral/ethical absolutes results in behavior that has severe consequences and can lead to special needs and dependence? For example, unmarried child bearing usually demands various types of governmental assistance.

Is it not true that the "new morality" creates a dependent class? Could it be that those favoring enlarging central government and coincidentally their own personal power, *want a* dependent class, and *need* a dependent class? Do they want a constituency that is willing to surrender freedom in order to get the care and guardianship they have been tricked into needing? Have these elitists rejected the ideal of their followers reaching their full potential and independence? Rather, do they desire to keep their followers in a state of want and dependency so they can increase their own power, influence and/or ensure their own employment or political position?

---

[31] Will & Ariel Durant, *The Lessons of History*;; (MJF Books N.Y. 1968) Pp.37, 51

A Shift - Not an Abandonment

Although there has been a shift of emphasis in absolutes in our culture, there has not been an overall reduction of them. The doctrine of being politically correct has introduced a vast number of "new" absolutes. Radical egalitarianism, multiculturalism and pluralism demand adherence to innumerable standards, rigid requirements and firm prohibitions. The espousing of absolutes is not an "old fashioned" or outmoded practice. It is very much in vogue. "Just the names have been changed to protect the innocent." If anything, the new morality (or immorality) is more unyielding in its demands, more severe in condemnation, more legalistic in it's forced behavior. It is indeed hypocritical and absurd to abhor the intolerance of so-called "Victorian" morality, while demanding absolute submission to the new morality of the political correct elitists.

Practically all of my adult life, I have been a police officer. I am very cautious about trying something that may sound good in theory but does not work in the real world. In my chosen profession, trying an unproven theory may result in someone's injury or death. I am interested in using absolutes that have been time tested. I believe it is dangerous to experiment with absolutes that are in vogue or part of a "pop culture." A new set of absolutes can look really good for a while. In theory they may seem to be liberating or empowering. But many do not "wear well". The true test of any absolute is it's long term impact.

The eight ethics we have discussed are ancient ones that have survived thousands of years of trial and error. I believe they are the type that the Durants found crossing cultural and time barriers.

A Clear Eye Toward History

A wise person will carefully examine ethics that have been validated throughout recorded history. We do not have to reinvent the wheel. Should we capriciously reject those principles that have proven effective and functional by those who have gone on before us? Shouldn't we be willing to learn through the experience of others? I strongly believe that we should not turn an arrogant blind eye to history.

The composition of one's absolutes is a choice. They are formed or revised by an act of the will. That being the case, a leader may decide to adopt or affirm those ethics that will help him or her reach their full potential. He/she can set a new standard for his/her own character development.

We are not born equal. You and I have a certain amount of athletic skills. But there are others undoubtedly endowed with more athletic skills than us and some who have less. Our potentials athletically are not equal. The same holds true with intellectual, musical and many other abilities. But in one respect we all have the same potential. We all have the same potential for developing our character. It is a matter of choice, commitment and determination.

Summary

Those who want to consistently demonstrate effective leadership behavior must embrace the ethics or character traits that support them. The ethics can be viewed as valuable solely due to their utility; or they can be accepted as both practical and morally right. Those who choose to accept ethics as absolutes and virtuous will be more likely to defend them, share them and take a stand for them. The composition of one's absolutes is a choice.

Action Steps:
- Think through your position on the issue of the character traits or ethics presented in this book. Do you accept them as valid?
- If you accept the eight leadership ethics as valid, what is your reason for doing so? Do you accept them strictly on the basis of their utilitarian value, or do you also appreciate their morality?
- Think through your core values or worldview. Determine what you believe regarding some of the basic issues of life. Determine how commitment to your core beliefs can support your leadership style.

In the next chapter we will examine ten ancient "absolutes" that have been used by many civilizations as requirements for social interaction.

Chapter 17
<u>Ten Ancient Principles</u>

Many authors have commented on the foolishness of turning a blind eye toward history. One of the most well known quotes on this issue is the statement: "Those who do not learn from history are bound to repeat it." Yet, although cautions about ignoring history abound, most of us disregard its valuable lessons. We seem helplessly programmed to repeat the mistakes of the past.

The principles contained in the "Ten Commandments" have been documented for over four thousand years. Many of the principles supporting the specific prohibitions occur in other ancient writings such as the "Code of Hamurabi" and the sayings of Confucius. Therefore they have been time tested. We have a wealth of historical facts to act as a matrix for their evaluation and assessment.

Secondly, they have been adopted as a moral consensus by many different societies over these many years. Their principles seem to apply to a variety of cultural, racial and geographic settings. They do not appear to be restricted in their successful application.

When societies have valued them, embraced them and used them as the basis to describe their social norms and prohibitions, they have become an inner compass to the members of those societies.

Principle #1: Authority

This principle addresses the whole issue of legitimate authority. In the ancient Torah it is stated as: "You shall have no other Gods before me." The basic principle here is Loyalty. In chapter 7 we addressed the practical aspects of loyalty being a necessary ethic in the life of a leader. In a real sense when one chooses to submit to the *legitimate* authority above them, they get under the flow of authority and actually become endowed with authority themselves.

Many people of faith choose to acknowledge God as the ultimate authority. I believe this is a very significant decision. I have found that when one chooses to acknowledge God as the ultimate authority a plethora of by-products occur. Life takes on meaning and a transcendent purpose can emerge. Accountability attaches to motivate the individual to place more importance on doing what is right and ethical. A leader in this group often places more weight on the ultimate "good" for his/her sphere of influence.

People of faith should recognize that God works through a chain of command. This means they submit to the immediate authority placed over them unless that authority demands they violate one of the other nine ancient principles (this is how we choose to define "legitimate authority").

This principle has application to those who choose not to believe in God as well; although in my opinion not as powerfully. People in this category should submit to the highest legitimate authority they recognize. For example, a colonel must recognize the authority of his/her general; a company vice president – his/her CEO, a child – his/her parent.

Loyalty acted out in submission to legitimate authority fosters order and stability in an organization or society. Understanding the importance of the flow of authority can clear up confusion, destructive infighting and on the positive side empower those who apply this principle.

Action Step: Submit to legitimate authority

Principle #2: Selflessness

This principle is the antithesis of egocentrism. It speaks to the notion of pursuing altruistic motives behind one's decisions. In the ancient Torah it forbid idols or man made Gods. It prohibited allowing anything to become a "god" and distract from a life of true worship. The basic principle here is to not allow a selfish ambition to become a "god."

For example, to many people money has become a god. By that I mean that the focal point of most decisions becomes financial. The question: "what is in this for me financially"? becomes an important criterion. Many parents have allowed the "god" of material success to destroy their effectiveness as a parent. Governmental leaders have allowed their "god" of personal ambition to make them corrupt rather than truly serve the people. Following this ancient principle would create a climate reducing corruption and the abuse or neglect of the followers. Rather it supports leadership that elevates altruism or noble motivation rather than a self made god.

Action Step: Develop a spirit of service to others

Principle #3: Keep Commitments

At the time of the establishment of these ancient principles, there were no such things as escrow papers or lengthy written contracts. Agreements on important issues needed some type of formal solemnization. Often the name of God was used to demonstrate a solemn and binding commitment. It was similar to our use of God's name to complete an oath of office or to testify truthfully in a court of law.

The Torah commanded that the name of God not be taken in vain. This meant that God's name was not to be used lightly. If his name was used to "swear" to an agreement – that the agreement be fulfilled. Today, many people apply this principle narrowly to forbidding profanity. Profanity by using God's name is of course included in this principle. But the basic principle goes much further than that. Historically, in ancient civilizations like Israel, God's name was used to formalize an agreement or commitment. For example, if two patriarchs intended to exchange property, they would go before the elders of the city and declare their intentions. Rather than signing a document they would "swear" in the name of God to fulfill their agreement.

The whole idea of keeping commitments has been trivialized and neglected. An application of this principle today would completely change the interaction of people both in business and private affairs. If solemn commitments were honored and fulfilled, the need for litigation would be dramatically reduced. This ancient principle is as relevant today as it was when first documented.

Action Step: Keep your commitments.

Principle #4: Balance

This principle has to do with maintaining a balance between work and rest. The original specific command was to "remember the Sabbath – to keep it holy." This originally required dedicating an entire day to rest, devote oneself to honoring God and enjoying family. Many legalistic requirements proliferated over the years. Some people reacted against what they viewed as unrealistic mandates. In my opinion the proverbial "baby was thrown out with the bath water." The basic principle is sound. Allowing one's life to get out of balance can have devastating results.

In my opinion, even people of faith almost universally neglect this ancient principle. The western world is a fast paced, success-oriented society. Materialism has distorted the reality of most of us. Our work ethic and achievement orientation can easily lead us to a state of imbalance. Rest, recreation and building healthy relationships can be neglected. Likewise focusing only on the material world can lead to a neglect of the intangible aspects of life. The aesthetic and spiritual dimensions of life can bring great fulfillment and peace.

Action Step: Evaluate your need to adjust your schedule and balance your life.

Principle #5: Honor Age and Experience

This principle put value on seniority and experience. Literally the ancient command was to "Honor your father and mother so that you may have a long life." The basic idea was to show respect and gratitude to the ones that in most cases have made the greatest contribution to one's life. Additionally it recognized the fact that wisdom can be accrued through many years of experiences.

It is my opinion that the reference to long life does not focus on chronological age, but rather the quality of life that one has during their later years. The most powerful influence that a parent has on his/her children is the example they demonstrate to them. A young father who neglects or abandons his parents will probably experience that neglect by his own children. A story is told of a father who places his ailing parent in a cart and begins to take him into a wilderness. The father's young son asks where he is taking his grandparent. The father explains that the aged one is sick, non-productive and must be taken to a special place to die. The young child then asks if he can go along. The father refuses. The child demands that he must go. The father inquires why the son feels it is necessary to go along. The son replies: "So I will know where to take you, when you are old and unproductive."

In the western world, youth is worshipped. Here we are encouraged to do just the opposite. This ancient principle exhorts us to value age, experience and demonstrate gratitude for what we have received and learned from those who have gone on before us. The result is wisdom, tranquility and continuity.

Action Step: Determine how you can honor those who have made a positive contribution to your life.

Principle #6: Murder prohibited

This principle emphasizes the importance of all human life. The Torah commanded: "You shall not murder." The Hebrew word clearly implies the immoral taking of a life and does not conflict with the earlier instruction on capital punishment (Genesis 9:3) as a strong sanction to demonstrate the importance of this principle. Neither does it conflict with the clear endorsement of self-defense (Genesis 22:3). The command is specific but the context includes broader implications. I believe it prohibits placing a lesser status of any human life based upon race, gender, age or any other reason. It is inclusive. It does not seem to allow for any exceptions. For example, euthanasia, abortion and ethnic purging are prohibited.

Understanding the importance of life has many implications. Holding this principle high will result in many humanitarian mandates. People who sincerely believe in the sanctity of human life should be willing help the poor, provide for the sick, handicapped and other legitimate welfare issues.

Action Step: Become aware of your role in protecting those who depend upon your leadership and influence.

Principle #7 Marriage Fidelity

This principle addresses the importance of the family institution and sexual purity. The ancient command forbade sexual intimacy outside the bounds of marriage, stating: "you shall not commit adultery." During the so-called "sexual revolution" of the sixties, this principle was attacked with vigor. The freedom of sexual promiscuity was celebrated. Now we are experiencing the corrosive affects of that choice. High rates of children born out of wedlock, divorce, domestic violence, clinical depression, sexual transmitted disease (STD) are just a few of the consequences occurring.

The family is, in my opinion, the most important of all social institutions. Its primary mission is to prepare young human beings to become productive and compatible members of society. When the family does its job well, social problems are reduced to a minimum. Dysfunctional families breed criminals, parasites and unfulfilled, unhappy people. This is why commitment to marriage and family is the most solemn and important of all societal relationships. Clearly, violating the principle of marriage fidelity is a major factor in eroding the family institution.

When someone violates the most important commitment of marriage and family, he or she demonstrates a likelihood of violating other commitments. This understandably increases skepticism on the part of someone evaluating such a person. Embracing this ancient principle can be a powerful factor in nurturing marriages, promoting trust and strengthening the family. Strong, viable families have an immeasurable positive impact on society.

Action Step: Make a commitment to honor your family in all areas of your life.

Principle #8: Property Rights

This principle addresses the fundamental issue of property. For thousands of years it has been recognized that people have certain inalienable rights, including the right to own private property. The initial drafts of the preamble to the U.S. Constitution referred to the "inalienable rights of Life, Liberty and Property." Later drafts change the word "Property" to the phrase "the pursuit of happiness." Records of the development of that famous document show that the whole idea of private property was intended to be included in that phrase. It has only been in recent history that the political philosophy of communism and radical socialism has mistakenly attacked this important concept. The tragic experiment with this flawed logic during the last fifty years has validated the classic approach.

The ancient prohibition stated: "You shall not steal." Although very brief and specific this simple statement has many implications. It is implied that one has the right to private property. It demands that in order to maintain social stability, members of society should respect the right of fellow members to be secure with their property. I believe this goes far beyond just prohibiting theft. Clearly the implications of the principle behind the specific prohibition include such acts as trespassing, vandalism and encourage the granting of privacy. Many conflicts, both personal and corporate, involves the violation of this principle. Wars, crime, and probably a majority of personal conflict are the results of the violation of this principle.

Action Step: Make a personal decision not to take materials from your workplace or steal time from your employer.

Principle #9: Be truthful & honest

This principle emphasizes the importance of maintaining integrity in social interchange. The specific command was: "You shall not lie or bear false witness." The basic principle addresses truthfulness and complete honesty in personal and public discourse.

In the American "Wild West" of the nineteenth century, calling someone a "liar" often resulted in a deadly gunfight. On the frontier where formal means of resolving disputes were either unavailable or impractical, a man's word was an absolute necessity. Major commerce – the sale of thousands of head of beef –

was often consummated with a handshake. A person whose integrity was questionable could find it impossible to conduct the basic transactions of life. In today's world, adherence to this principle has very positive results. Honesty and integrity results in mutual trust, respect and compatibility.

Action Step: Seek to be straightforward and transparent in your contacts with others.

Principle #10: Be contented

This principle goes to the root of many social problems. The ancient command stated: "You shall not covet." This addresses a strong compulsion to want something that belongs to another(s). It implies envy, jealously and malice. It is the opposite of contentment. This pattern of thinking can be the root to illegal, immoral and unethical conduct. Corruption has its roots in covetousness.

This serious issue is not necessarily connected to one's possessions or lack thereof. It is possible to have many possessions and not be contented. It is also possible to have few possessions and be contented. Contentment is a state of mind.

I believe it is possible to have healthy ambition without violating this principle. Setting personal goals and working toward them does not necessarily involve envy. Having ambition will not automatically rule out contentment. Living in the present and being grateful for today's reality is an indication of contentment. Being consumed with the future to the neglect of the present is one of the indications of ignoring this principle. Set goals, prepare for the future; but enjoy the "now" and be grateful for what you have. This results in happiness – a very important condition that eludes many in our materialistic society.

Action Step: Develop a grateful spirit

Conclusions:

The major reason given for not publicly valuing these principles is that they are religious doctrine. I hope that I have demonstrated here that the principles may be discussed and taught in a secular context and setting. I have not referred to a church or religion in this chapter. Even though myself a "man of faith", I have attempted to show the application of the principles to people who choose not to believe in God.

What would our society be like if these ancient time tested principles were valued? It seems obvious that everyone would benefit. The family would be strengthened. Litigation would be reduced. Conflicts between individuals and groups would shrink. Mutual respect would increase. In short, we would all have a greater potential for peace, healing, stability and happiness.

Leadership: The Power of Character

Chapter 18
The Spiritual Dimension of Leadership

I want to be the type of leader I have described in this book. I have not yet arrived at that ideal. It is a very difficult road to walk. The road is steep with many curves and hazards. Some say it is an impossible journey -- "that you can't get there from here." In one sense, I agree. It does seem impossible. But I have found, with many others, the potential for "fighting the good fight -- finishing the course." I am convinced there is a way to approach this ideal. It involves the concept of "**Balance**."

Losing or not maintaining balance in one's life can be destructive or limit one achieving their full potential. For example, spending a disproportionate amount of time at work in comparison to family or physical fitness activities can result in severe health problems or a dysfunctional family. Balance in life is an important concept.

World View

We have discussed one's core values and worldview. I believe an individual's worldview can have a profound impact on this most important "balancing act." If a person looks upon himself as biological accident, without any divine or eternal purpose, he/she will be likely to reject the possibility of the existence of absolutes. He/she will look upon ethics or morals as being relative, flexible and man made. This is not only understandable, it should be expected. If there is no God, then there is no "right" or "wrong." If there is no God, then there is no plan; there are no absolutes.

Such a person will also view himself as self sufficient, without any need for "outside" help. Often they view those who do acknowledge a Supreme Being as weak and needing a "crutch." Typically, they are very confident and independent to an extreme.

On the other hand, those of us who believe in a creative God will search for meaning in life. Once a person crosses the threshold of choosing to believe in a creator there are many implications that arise. If we are the products of a creative act then are we not accountable to that creator? If we are tangible evidence to an intricate design (and I believe we are), then can we not expect to find some absolutes in that design and plan? Moreover, should we not pursue knowledge about this creator?

World View & Leadership

This discussion of one's world view or core beliefs is relevant to leadership for two important reasons. First, one's worldview is related to their position on "absolutes." If one chooses the worldview that acknowledges God, their logic will eventually lead them to accept the notion of His order, His will, and His absolutes. At some point they must deal with accountability to Him and His absolutes. In other words, the existence of God and the notion of absolutes are related. As mentioned before, when ethics are viewed as moral or "right" (i.e. absolutes) in addition to merely functional, there will exist a stronger and lasting commitment to them. In summary, worldview is related to absolutes; and absolutes are related to the leadership ethic of conviction and the capacity to inspire.

If a person recognizes that they exist because a creator brought them into being, then it is natural and logical to become interested in the purpose of that act. It is understandable and to be expected that they will want to know more about the plan of the creator. They will search for His precepts and His guidance. They will be open to the notions of purpose, absolutes and destiny.

Secondly, an awareness of God will place in one's very being what some philosophers have described as a "God Shaped Vacuum." When this occurs, the potential for a complete personal renewal is within reach. A personal relationship with God can unleash the potential for a great inner strength to act out the ethics one has adopted or renewed. The embracing of moral absolutes, coupled with an inner spiritual strength is a very powerful duo that enables one to act out their belief system

The complexity of man

I agree with many philosophers and theologians that man is a very complex being. He is not a biological accident. He is the product of an incredible design and purpose. He is a being with three distinct components. First we are physical -- we have a body that allows us to interact with the physical world. Secondly, we are intellectual. We have a soul or psyche that allows us to interact with other people. Finally, we are spiritual. We have the potential to interact with God. This is where balance comes in. I believe a person who achieves balance with these three entities has greater potential for achieving excellence, fulfillment and significance.

The Earth Suit

I once heard a speaker refer to the human body as an "earth suit." I believe this is a brilliant metaphor. It describes our bodies as containers of "The Self." It recognizes that there is something about a human being that transcends the collection of minerals and water that technically make up the body. It suggests that there is something more - a *person* lives in that body. Having said that, I must emphasize that our bodies are an important part of our existence. We must care for them or suffer consequences. The consequences can have a profound impact on the other two components of our lives.

A well-balanced person understands the importance of his/her "earth suit" and devotes appropriate attention to nutrition, exercise and the overall upkeep of it. An efficiently functioning body allows the inhabitant to move around successfully in the physical realm. Fortunately, in recent years much attention has been focused on physical fitness and so-called "wellness." There seems to be more of an awareness of the importance of "earth suit" maintenance. Nurturing your "earth suit" is wise.

The Soul

The soul has been defined as the *immaterial essence* of a human life. The whole concept of the soul, psyche or "self" recognizes that there is someone behind the eyeballs. The word *soul* puts a label on the personality, life or intellect that resides in the body. As the material body enables us to interact with other material things - the physical world, the soul enables us to interact with other intellectual beings - other souls. We can establish connections with other persons in the arena of ideas, opinions, emotions, commitments and dreams.

A well-balanced person will nurture his/her soul or self. Just as it is important to care for one's body, it is also important to provide nutrients and exercise to one's intellect. A wise person deliberately exposes himself/herself to learning experiences. They cherish the disciplines of education and training. They read literature that challenges their intellectual development. They seek relationships that expand their perspective. The development of the intellectual component of the total person allows that person to move around successfully in the intellectual sphere of life.

The Spirit

The spiritual side of man is more difficult to address. Yet this dimension of existence has profound implications and significance. The words *spirit* and *soul are* often interchanged. Yet, even in their formal definitions they are distinct and different. Definitions of *spirit involve* words like "ecclesiastical", "religious" and "supernatural." Clearly the word *spirit implies* a component of man that may transcend this world. I hold to this position.

As the body allows contact with the physical world, and the soul allows contact in the intellectual realm, I believe the spirit is designed to allow contact with the spiritual world -- contact with the creator God.

In the recent past, science has made it difficult for an intellectual person to be open minded about the existence of God. However recently the discussion of the so-called anthropic principle has turned the tables.

> The burden of proof has shifted. The barrier that modern science appeared to erect to faith has fallen. Of course the anthropic principle tells us nothing about the Person of God or the existence of an afterlife; it has nothing to say about such issues as right or wrong or the "problem of evil." But it does offer as strong an indication as reason and science alone could be expected to provide that God exists. [32]

I have strong spiritual convictions. Readers interested in those specific beliefs may choose to examine Appendix I (following this chapter). I have documented these beliefs because I believe in "full disclosure."

From belief to action

Recently, I realized the fulfillment of a secret fantasy. For many years I've wanted to experience a catapult take-off from an U.S. aircraft carrier warship. Yet, when I was offered the opportunity to actually go through this somewhat risky venture, I hesitated. Carrier landings and take-offs do involve some danger. After I gave some thought to the trade-offs, I decided this incredible opportunity was worth the risk.

We flew from the North Island Naval Air Station in San Diego to the U.S.S. Constellation. This great ship was involved in training exercises off the coast of California. As we approached the battle fleet, the carrier was easy to identify. Although it was large in comparison to the other ships, it seemed smaller than I expected. One Navy aviator, clearly "pulling my chain," explained that on the landing approach " . . .they look about the size of a tombstone." The landing was breathtaking . . . and abrupt. They call it, " A controlled crash."

During my three-day stay, I observed nearly a hundred take-offs and landings. I watched legendary F-14 "Tomcats", high tech F-18 "Hornets" and A-6 "Intruders" and their near twin, radar jamming "Prowlers" do their stuff. The experience gave me great admiration and appreciation for the professionalism and diligence of the men and women of the United States Navy. Living with them

---

[32] God: The evidence; Patrick Glynn; Prima Publishing 1997

Leadership: The Power of Character

for just those three days gave me an understanding of the sacrificial commitment they must have.

I must admit, when it was time to leave, I had some reservations in my mind about the catapult take-off. I realized that there was some danger involved. Earlier I noted that the first aircraft launched was a rescue helicopter that hovered off the starboard bow. Their job was to rescue survivors in the event of an unsuccessful take-off. That was sobering. Then I was briefed on emergency procedures should we "hit the deck." Earlier the "X.O." (Executive Officer), "Bear" Pickavance, had explained that we would accelerated from zero to 180 MPH in 2 to 3 seconds. The "G" forces would be great.

I believed all the right things. I had been watching with admiration the naval aviation operations on the carrier for three days. I was a true believer. I believed that the aircraft would fly. I believed the steam catapult would fire. I believed the aviator was skilled. But, at the moment of truth -- when I walked across the flight deck to climb into the aircraft -- I realized there was a difference between belief and faith. Belief can be an intellectual exercise. Belief can be impersonal. Belief does not necessarily involve commitment. On the other hand, faith is personal and must involve commitment. In fact, faith is taking a belief to the point of commitment.

In my situation on the carrier deck, faith involved sufficiently believing in all of the elements of an aircraft carrier take-off to take the action of getting in the aircraft and personally experiencing the take off.

Well, I did. I did get aboard. The catapult fired. We were rocketed into the air. The acceleration was literally breathtaking. Then suddenly we were at the end of the deck. The firm powerful drive of the catapult abruptly ceased. The air felt spongy as the aircraft sort of wafted down slightly. It felt as though we were slowing down, although I later learned we were still accelerating - just at a lower rate. At that precise moment I realized we were committed.

Most people believe in God. Surveys in the United States by respected polling firms consistently reveal that over 90 % of Americans indicated a belief in God or a Supreme Being. But as I have illustrated, belief can be impersonal. It does not always involve commitment. Having a personal relationship with God must involve faith. It is personal. It involves action.

Transforming my belief in the carrier take-off into faith involved climbing aboard the aircraft. As a follower of Jesus, transforming my belief in Him into faith involved my inviting his Spirit into my life. It involved a step of commitment - a prayer of submission to Him. [33] And that prayer began the relationship. It opened the vault to the vast resources of God.

If you are open to the concept of the spiritual man, then I encourage you to pursue that dimension of life. I have found direction, significance, and the inner strength I believe is necessary to approach the ideals I have presented in this book.

Elevate your dreams - your ambitions - from success to significance. Leave a noble legacy. Make a difference. Believe in something. Care about something. Have the courage to take a stand for something. Be a leader.

"And you will seek Me and find Me, when you search for Me with all your heart." Jeremiah Circa 500 BC [34]

---

[33] The New American Standard Bible: (Foundation Press, La Habra, CA. 1960) The Gospel of John 1:12;

[34] The New American Standard Bible:; (Foundation Press, La Habra, CA. 1960) Jeremiah 29:13

Leadership: The Power of Character

Appendix I
Outline of author's beliefs

As a "follower of Jesus", I believe in the basics of his Gospel. I believe: (1) that man was created with all three of his components (Body, soul and spirit) functioning perfectly, (2) that our ancestors were given the status of a "free moral agent" - the autonomy to choose to follow the Creator's limits or disobey, (3) that they chose to disobey - to sin, (4) that as warned by the creator God, the result of that disobedience was death, (5) that the death was a spiritual death - a separation from God, (6) that as a result, every human from that point on entered the experience of life with only two of his/her three basic components functioning - a body and a soul with a nonfunctioning or dead spirit. I believe this is the reason that Jesus coined the phrase "Born Again."

In the scripture Jesus is quoted as responding to an Israeli intellectual that he needed to be 'Born again." (The Gospel of John Chapter 3). When this intellectual (Nicodemus) reacted with shock and confusion about a second birth of his body, Jesus made it clear that he needed a spiritual rebirth that he was not talking about the body. He announced that was the reason of his appearance on earth. He explained that He came to make it possible for a spiritual quickening for each one choosing to follow Him.

I believe the Gospel as described in the Bible. I believe: (1) that Jesus is the son of God, born miraculously without a human father, (2) that he lived a perfect and exemplary life, (3) that he willingly died a substitutionary death for us, to pay the penalty of our sin, (4) that he was resurrected from death and lives today, (5) and that all who choose to confess their sin (agree with God that they are not perfect like Him) and turn from their own way, receiving Him as their savior and Lord are reborn spiritually. That is, the Spirit of God comes to dwell within them, thus giving them spiritual life.

When I made this life changing decision, I prayed three prayers that I believe are taught in the Bible.

(1) **The Prayer of Confession:** This first step means admitting to God that you are not perfect like Him; and therefore are a sinner. The Bible states: "For all have sinned, and fall short of the glory of God" (Romans 3:23). The phrase "fall short" explains how God classifies sinners. All who fall short of His perfection are "sinners". I know that I am not perfect like God. I have found that many people have a problem with this because it is so humbling. This prayer is described in I John, Chapter 1 verse 9 (in the Bible).

(2) **The Prayer of repentance**: Repentance means a change of direction. It means turning from one thing to another. Jesus spoke often of the necessity of this action. This prayer is centered on our willingness to turn from "our own way" to the Lord, who alone is able to make us into the people He wants us to be. The Bible says we must turn to God and seek His help in being the person He wants us to be (Acts chapter 26 verse 20). Many people who believe in the Lord have not repented. Many do ask for God's help when they experience difficulties. But they do not "turn" to him. Rather they ask the Lord to come join them as they continue going their own way. I became willing to turn from my own way. This was a significant step for me.

(3) **The Prayer of Commitment**: There is a difference between belief and trust. The Bible says: "He came unto His own creation; but His own received Him not. But as many as received Him, to them He gave the power to become the sons of God." (The Gospel of John, chapter 1, verse 12). This prayer is taking one's belief in the Lord to the point of commitment. It means inviting the Lord Jesus to come into your life.

When I prayed these prayers, He came into my life and gave me a spirit -- His Holy Spirit. This is what Jesus meant when He said we must "be born again".

If you pray these prayers sincerely, God will come into your life also. You will have spiritual life. But this new spiritual life is similar to physical life. It needs to grow and be nurtured. Just as there are three food groups for the physical body, there are three essentials of spiritual growth.

(1) Bible Study: The Word of God (Bible) is to the spirit as food is to the body. Begin reading the bible. I recommend starting with the Gospel of John. Pray before each reading. Ask God to help you understand. Find a church that teaches the Bible (not all do) and begin attending.

(2) Prayer: Begin talking to God. That is prayer. Be grateful to Him for His many gifts. Express your deepest needs and fears. Ask Him for strength, help and wisdom.

(3) Fellowship: Begin talking with someone who also has this commitment. The Bible teaches us that we need one another for encouragement, support and accountability.

I have experienced this process. I am experiencing the presence of the Spirit of God in my life and all that results from that decision. I am experiencing God's forgiveness for my sin, His guidance, His comfort and His peace. I am also learning to draw on the bank of His promise to give me the inner strength I need to be the man He designed me to be. I have a personal relationship with God.

Robert L. Vernon, January 2013
chiefrlv@aol.com

www.ingramcontent.com/pod-product-compliance
Lightning Source LLC
Chambersburg PA
CBHW080244180526
45167CB00006B/2410